Life beyond Spending

Spend Less, and Live More

Ernesto Caravantes

Hamilton Books
A member of
ROWMAN & LITTLEFIELD
Lanham • Boulder • New York • Toronto • Plymouth, UK

Hamilton Books
4501 Forbes Boulevard
Suite 200
Lanham, Maryland 20706
Hamilton Books Acquisitions Department (301) 459-3366

10 Thornbury Road
Plymouth PL6 7PP
United Kingdom

Printed in the United States of America
British Library Cataloging in Publication Information Available

Library of Congress Control Number: 2013945699
ISBN: 978-0-7618-6204-8 (paperback : alk. paper)
eISBN: 978-0-7618-6205-5

™ The paper used in this publication meets the minimum requirements of American National Standard for Information Sciences—Permanence of Paper for Printed Library Materials, ANSI Z39.48-1992

This book is dedicated to all who were affected by the Recession of 2008.

CONTENTS

PART I

Reflections on Life beyond Spending

This book is about slavery. However, this is not slavery in the ordinary sense of physical servitude. Although the physical form of slavery has disappeared, there is a new form of slavery, and it is quite insidious. This new slavery is all around us. This slavery is just as real as the chains that were once used to force people to be servants. However, instead of wrought iron chains, the chains that I am referring to are inside of us. These chains have become part of our inner selves. And, worse yet, we have allowed these mental chains to be placed upon us.

No one has forced us to become the slaves that we have become. This was voluntary. And, yet, the effects of this form of slavery can be quite self-destructive. The slavery being referred to here is the bondage to a lifestyle of compulsive consumption. In a broader sense, the slavery at issue here is the unrelenting desire people have for material goods and the length to which this attachment to purchases dominates so many people's lives. This book will challenge readers to identify their own possible slavery to spending and to the empty promise that corporate America gives us that a given purchase will bring happiness.

So many of us get caught into the mental trap of thinking that, as my pastor once said it, "Happiness is just a purchase away." We feel that once we acquire that long sought-after home, or car, or set of skis, that we will finally be happy or fulfilled. Of course, no one can deny that there are some very nice items being sold in the corporate world. Beautiful silk suits or candy apple-red sports cars. They are very nice, and they have their appeal. Yet, what this book attempts to point out is the relentless pursuit of these items.

Countless people work very hard at their jobs their whole lives in order to attain some of these toys. Of course, one can come up with a few counterpoints, such as: they did not steal these items – they worked hard for the money to purchase them. No theft or bribery was involved. Secondly, one could argue that they are entitled to enjoy these things. After all, we are not referring to drugs, or something which is harmful or self-destructive. These are innocent purchases. And, there is some validity to these statements. Heaven knows that I have purchased more than a couple of items, and many of them were purchased with the same expectation that the item would make me happy. Indeed, some of the purchases did make me happy.

Therefore, one could argue, if the author himself admits to giving in to the wish to purchases items (usually clothing) that he felt would make him happy, and which, furthermore, did make him happy, then what's the problem? I also did things the right way and worked hard and saved my money, and then treated myself to some goodies which I felt would make welcome additions to my life. To the untrained eye, it may seem like I am speaking out of both sides of my mouth. Yet, there is a critical distinction that must be made.

I have made purchases which I felt would make me happy. Yet, these were purchases that I alone wanted to make. There was no exterior motivation, other than the fact that some of these clothes were in season and were being advertised in the media. Yet, even that was not exterior 'motivation.' That was only the visual reference point that I used in making my decision to purchase the CDs or shirts that I ended up with. No one encouraged me to give in and purchase them.

Furthermore, I was not in competition with anyone else in making my decision. One of my colleagues once admitted to me that when a colleague at her job purchased a certain type of SUV, she felt compelled to compete and ended up buying one that was bigger and better. This is the type of mental slavery that I am referring to in this tome. It is the compulsion to make a purchase based upon society's demands. There is truly nothing wrong in wanting a pretty blouse, or a nice leather wallet. However, the critical distinction is that if you decide to make the purchase, you should make sure that you are buying it for all the right reasons. It is akin to the decision to get married. There is certainly nothing wrong in getting married. Weddings are truly beautiful ceremonies, and they rank among my absolute favorite rituals to watch. Marriage is a timeless and wonderful institution. Therefore, no one is going to see anything wrong in two people getting married.

The problems lie when the decision to get married is made for all the wrong reasons. So many people have married their partner in the hopes that marriage will ensure that the partner will remain forever faithful and committed. This, of course, backfires, and the partner ends up leaving anyway. Or, it may be a shotgun wedding. In those instances, an accident has occurred, one which was not planned, and the baby will suffer as a result. Therefore, in a sense, weddings are beautiful rites of passage, but sometimes used for the wrong reasons. If both partners truly love each other, and possess the deepest respect for each other, then there is little problem. The problem lies when the decision to get married is made because of outer, rather than inner reasons.

Furthermore, the decision to get married has to be an inner and *healthy* reason. Therefore, with respect to purchases, if a certain CD, or book will make you happy, and it is something you have always wanted to have, then by all means, treat yourself to it. But, if you are trying to keep up with the Joneses, then you are making a purchase for the wrong reason. I remember speaking to someone who had a friend in her 50s, and she said to me how surprising she found it that her friend didn't "own property" at that stage in her life. I later questioned her about her statement. I found it to be judgmental and unfair. She agreed and later retracted her statement.

However, the implication was quite clear. We are "expected" to own certain things, like property, at a certain age in our lives. If we do not own property but rather, rent property, we are then questioned. There must be something wrong if we don't own property! We must have failed somehow. Our ambitions in life were not high enough. We did not strive as much as we *should* have. However, therein lies the insidiousness of this social phenomenon. It is the set of values that so many people have become enslaved to, and which they never question. Let us examine this more closely. If a person, in his or her 50s doesn't own property, but is renting a home, where is the problem? If the individual is employed and works, as we all should, and works diligently, and, from the earnings, pays the rent on time, as well as the other usual bills and expenses, where is the failing? Why is the ownership of property such an enduring metric?

And, even if a person were to make enough money such that he or she could pay a mortgage each month, yet prefers the trouble-free (almost) lifestyle of the renter, then that is a choice that should never be judged. Yet, we have allowed ourselves to culturally inherit these arbitrary and somewhat Puritanical standards to such an extent that we no longer take time to question them. Of course, none of this came by accident. There is a reason that things are the way they are in our society.

For three hundred years, America has held onto what has been referred to as the Protestant Ethic, and some have referred to it as the Protestant *Work* Ethic. This has its roots deep in Protestant theology. Early Protestants in Europe felt that human beings were born into membership of either the Elect, or the Damned. If you were a member of the Elect, you were saved, and were guaranteed front-row seats in the Kingdom of God. If, however, you were one of the Damned, there wasn't much you could do to save yourself.

It was all like some grand religious lottery, and it was always hoped for that you were among those with the golden Wonka Bar one-way ticket to Heaven. Yet, while on Earth, there was no real or true guarantee that you might be one of the elect. It was truly luck of the draw. Yet, among many Protestants, there appeared the idea that the more one accomplished, and the more one accumulated in terms of material wealth in life, the more these might be signs of being a member of the Elect.

There was no way of truly knowing for sure, but if one got to the end of one's life with a financial empire, including property and wealth to pass down to one's progenitors, then it might very well be a sign that you were among the saved. It would be obvious – how could all of this good fortune have happened were it not for the fact that you were one of saved? Surely, the fact that God had given you all of this wealth must be a sign that you were one of saved. Why else would this have happened? However, times changed and some of the values in society changed. The Enlightenment came along, and, with it, the desire to see things in rational terms, rather than a religious paradigm. Natural events, such as the appearance of comets, or earthquakes, were now seen in a new light. It was no longer an angry God who brought down thunder, but, rather it was an electrical event.

Therefore, natural science was filling the void that was left behind by the absence of religion. Science became the new religion, and some of our country's founders became icons of this new Age of Reason, such as Benjamin Franklin and Thomas Jefferson. Yet, as important and as far-reaching as this new paradigm was for human history, there were some vestiges of the older Protestant view of life. The view that "he who dies with the most toys wins" endured well into the modern age. Those words were not chosen capriciously by me to make a point. Those words were on a bumper sticker that I have seen more than once. Yet, that bumper sticker speaks volumes. That bumper sticker is not funny, or even amusing to me. Perhaps I would be amused were it not for the fact that those words are accompanied by an entire culture built around acquiring toys, and the idea that he who has the most material possessions wins.

I have always wanted to ask "Wins what?" Is this a race? Is this a competition? And, unfortunately, the answer is yes. We are caught up in a social competition. And it shapes the values that we hold dear. One single man told me that in his community, when he makes advances on single women and makes his interest known to her, the first thing women ask him is: "What sort of car do you drive?" This has become such an entrenched way of thinking that we don't question it at all. This 'race' or 'competition' in which we find ourselves has become a complete distortion of what may have been (at one point) a set of values which honored hard work and which placed a premium on saving money. After all, the early Protestants valued frugality and looked down upon conspicuous consumption. The original statutes of some of the early universities in America, such as Harvard and Yale, forbade the wearing of showy or "proud" colors in the undergraduates. They were ordered to wear plain black robes.

It has been written that when Increase Mather, one of the early Puritan ministers in New England, went to Trinity College in Ireland to complete his education, he found himself surrounded by the other students wearing multi-colored robes for their graduation. Instead, in true Puritan form, he wore a plain black robe for the commencement ceremony. Yet, somewhere in history, this Puritan ideal became distorted or twisted out of shape. Rather than maintaining a distaste, or restriction, on proud or bright colors, our American consciousness shifted to one of conspicuous wealth.

Homes and mansions became bigger and bigger. It was as though there was an "unspoken race" or competition which commenced. And, it seems that in this race, it became absolutely necessary that every contestant demonstrate, at one point or another, how much one had accumulated in terms of property, land, money, slaves, or horses. It was some kind of badge of merit that one could wear with pride. It was a kind of club, and in order to be a member of this club, one had to descend from Old Money, and one had to have a lot of this Old Money invested well, and invested in an opulent fashion. It became somehow necessary to announce to the world how much money you owned. It was not enough to have it, but to flaunt it as well. Therein lies the beginning of the mentality of competitive consumption around which this book's concern revolves. A culture was built around this flaunting of wealth. Perhaps I would not have begun to carry on my crusade as much as I have had the "culture of flaunted wealth" ended centuries ago. It is the fact that all of society has continued to embrace this mentality that concerns me. No one has truly questioned this paradigm.

Yet, there are signs of hope. The recession that began in 2008, and the subsequent economic collapse that accompanied it, has caused scores of enlightened Americans to stop and take stock. Perhaps this questioning of values in society was already percolating in the back of our national consciousness and all it took was mere "nudging" from the recession to cause it to fall firmly in place. Yet, I do see the signs that society is beginning to sober up from the drunken party of blind material accumulation. And, part of the process of becoming sober is to take stock of what has happened and why it happened. Of course, nothing is as simple as it seems. There were many factors contributing to the economic collapse which began in 2008 and which, as of this writing, is still being felt. I think that people are beginning to realize that there is more to life than the accumulation of things bought on credit. There is more to life than dying with a lot of "toys." However, this realization is a long time in coming.

It took the economic crisis to bring out in people a sensibility which should have been there at the start. People are hungering for more than just a new purchase or a new car. I believe that there is a genuine spiritual hunger in America. Only a return to a simpler way of life can bring about the true satisfaction of this appetite. And, this book ultimately serves to salute those who have taken that leap of faith, so to speak. It takes true bravery, and true independence, to question societal values that are three hundred years old and to begin sculpting a new paradigm. This process has, at its roots, the beginning of a noble enterprise which aims to replace one set of unhealthy values for another, healthier set of values. In a sense, what has happened is that many citizens began to realize that they were enslaved, and eventually wanted to throw the shackles off and start a new life. Ultimately, this book is dedicated to them.

Yet, this has not been a total victory, and there is a real and deep-seated reason for this. There is a difference in realizing that one can no longer afford to live above one's means and actually questioning the cultural values that encouraged financial debt in the first place. This book will be exploring this critical distinction. Not many people understand the diametrical separateness between these two concepts. It is not difficult to calculate a budget and to look at one's income and expenses. It doesn't take long for one to be able to discern whether one is spending more than one is earning.

Of course, budgets are important. Budgets allow one to see how money is being spent or saved. In a sense, budgets are a forgotten art as well as a science. They have a heuristic value and are quite informative. This, of course, presupposes that one is being honest in the representation of spending and saving within the budget. If one prepares a budget correctly, one can see very clearly where the money is going. A decision can then be made to both spend less, and save more, or to earn more money, or to borrow more. Yet, even a budget allows the values in society to remain without question. A budget does not *question the values* of society. Only people can do that.

All that a budget can do is to provide an alert to the fact that too much money is being spent, or that too little income is being saved. Thus, even if a person is adept at designing a budget, it will only allow a person to know if the pattern of spending in proportion to earning has to be readjusted. But, in a sense, the central problem, as it were, remains unsolved. The pivotal issue is the slavery to materialism that is so rampant in society. The press does little to help this situation. I read recently that a movie actress spent more than $170,000 on a brand new luxury automobile. Of course, one can dismiss these stories by rationalizing that someone in her position can afford to spend that kind of money. After all, she is probably a millionaire, so why shouldn't she spend that kind of money? But, again, the central issue is being avoided.

And yet, the manner in which the press joyfully publishes these articles demonstrates where society's values have become situated. The articles are not about talent, or the career trajectories of these movie stars, it's about what they own, and what they are purchasing, or how much money they have in the bank. This is what people ultimately want to know. Rather than seeing the money that movie stars have made as the inevitable result of successful movie making, the voyeuristic press is all too eager to publish *how* these people are going to spend their money. Let the movie critics provide their two cents about the artistic merit of movies, but what we really want to hear or read about is just how large so-and-so's mansion is, or how many sports cars late night television hosts own.

Television shows like *Lifestyles of the Rich and Famous* only add to the fascination and mystique that we attach to the world of the well-heeled and the heaps of material possessions that they are able to accumulate. This is the voyeurism that is gripping America. It's not the love life of celebrities, or even the sexual escapades that we want to know about. What really matters is the size of their palatial home, or the helipad on the back of a yacht and the slick helicopter which occupies it. This is the preoccupation. And, let's face it; it is quite impressive to see how people live in certain areas, such as the Hamptons, or the Berkshires, or Beverly Hills.

I certainly have been impressed with what I have seen on television shows, or in magazines. These McMansions, as they are now called, certainly have a stately appearance, and they do indeed provide every comfort imaginable. It's not hard to understand the reasons that people spend hours glued in front of their televisions, drooling at the images of the large palatial homes and luxurious lifestyles of the rich and famous. This kind of voyeurism has a kind of Disneyland-like appeal, like a visual vacation in which you get to forget the bills, and the shaky marriage, and the homework battles with the kids.

Instead of Cinderella's Castle, it's the castle of a movie star or celebrity. It's a world of breath-taking vistas, six-course meals, silk suits, limousine rides, and private jets. It definitely has its escape value. And the press serves up these images to the working class very enthusiastically, as if to say, "You see, if you work hard enough, or land upon some great amount of luck, all of this can be yours!" The poor or working class viewer of these gilded images can only sigh in a state of sad resignation, somehow convinced that the fortune necessary to purchase or to have those things will never materialize. They turn off the television, sigh again, wishing they could live that lifestyle, and go to sleep.

The next day, these same people face a job they probably don't enjoy and commiserate with their coworkers about how little they are paid, and in the back of their minds, they still hold onto that image of the palaces that they saw on television the night before, and it is this image that carries them throughout the day. One day, they tell themselves, I will have all of that, or at least some of it. That becomes the mantra that echoes and bounces around in their minds as they face their miserable days. Yet, something is terribly wrong with this picture.

No one questions the manner in which society operates. No one questions whether the materiel wealth they saw on the television the night before would actually make them happy. Would it solve any marital difficulties? Only if the difficulties in the marriage are related to money! Would having the limousine help a person with low self-esteem? Would having a private helicopter help someone who doesn't feel lovable? People conveniently forget that the lives of the rich and famous are not always immune to the same psychological difficulties that all of us face. Just a casual glance at the magazine articles at the checkout stands in supermarkets shows the unhappiness that movie stars and other celebrities face: divorces, three-day marriages, drug and alcohol addiction, and even suicide. In fact it seems that the more famous and rich they become, the worse their troubles get, or so it seems. However, those stories prove a point. Material wealth is not insurance against unhappiness. Someone very wise was once asked whether money takes away your problems, and the response was: No, it doesn't take away your problems, but it makes your surroundings much more comfortable while you contemplate your problems. I would agree with this assessment. Yet, a certain amount of physical comfort is the only thing that money can truly provide. Yet, money cannot protect us against cancer, heart attacks, infidelity, or the choice to use drugs. Yet, as a society, we have convinced ourselves that once we live in our palaces and have a limousine and a private jet, that life will somehow be magically free of problems or unhappiness.

Yet, the articles that I have read of celebrities prove just the opposite. As it has already been said, the more you own, the more time has to be spent in the upkeep and maintenance of your material items. The more you possess, the more time you have to devote to keeping track of, protecting, and even insuring, your goods. And one has to wonder, truly, at the logistics of the lives of some of these celebrities. Just how many sports cars can one drive in a day? Just how many airplanes does a person need to own? Is it not enough that persons with money can purchase perfectly comfortable seats in first-class on commercial airliners or first class cabins on cruise liners? Do they have to go and buy their own plane, or their own boat?

Those with lots of money have no wish, it seems, to associate or socialize with those "beneath" them. They must stand apart. They don't want to associate with the proletariat on a commercial airliner or a commercial cruise line. They purchase their own planes and boats so that they can isolate themselves. The wealthy want to be left alone, like Greta Garbo. Those that are rich want to "elevate" themselves into a social class that is all their own. Heaven forbid that they socialize with someone who is not at their social level, or that they befriend someone who doesn't have money.

This exclusivity, or this wish to be left alone, may be a clue as to why the rich and famous end up having their meltdowns and end up at the Betty Ford Clinic. Their wish to be left alone creates a world that is both lonely and empty. They end up, as one of my friends put it, with too much money and time on their hands. Idle hands may not be the Devil's workshop, but the idleness of the rich and famous seems to be what predisposes them to drugs, particularly the expensive ones, such as cocaine. Once people get to that level, they are absorbed into a world that is superficial. It is based on appearances. It is a world of glitz and glamor, but also of phoniness. Their money cannot disguise the unhappiness that the rich and famous feel. One can see it in their faces. Despite their ability to afford the top plastic surgeons in the country, they still age prematurely. If they are not committing themselves to detox centers, they are having affairs, or getting divorced, or all three. They have lost sight of who they are. And, perhaps, they have been using their fame and money to run from themselves, and to numb their emotional pain and feelings of emptiness. One need only to look at the tragic life of Michael Jackson in order to comprehend this phenomenon. That lifestyle ended up costing him his life.

One could come up with a counterargument and say that the working classes also end up as alcoholics, or drug addicts, or having affairs and getting divorced. It could be said that I am picking on the rich and famous, and that they are only human. It is true. They are only human, and they bleed and cry like the rest of us. Yet, my concern is based upon the fact that so many of us believe that once we have a certain amount of money, or a dream home, that we will be immune to life's problems. So many of us buy into (no pun intended) the belief that once we get the latest gadget or purchase that we desire, that our lives will be transformed. Some even believe that they will be a "new person." Change, that is, real change, can only come from the inside.

The decisions we make to truly enrich our lives cannot be guided by our appetites for material wealth. Happiness, as we all know, cannot be purchased. It cannot be bought in a store. It doesn't come from Amazon.com wrapped in a nice gift box and placed gently at our door. For example, someone wanting to connect to nature, or the divine, cannot purchase this experience. One could purchase a nice stereo set with CDs that play the sounds of nature, but is that a substitute for the experience of watching a sunset? One could purchase a nice and expensive coffee table book on the beauty of forests, but is that any substitute for actually wondering through a trail and smelling the moss from the trees and being able to hold their leaves in your hand?

Is there any commercial equivalent for standing in the middle of a clearing and feeling the spring rain tap gently on your face and roll down your cheeks and hair? Is there any substitute for holding a new born baby in your arms and being able to look into her eyes and truly feel the presence and love of God? Even a simple rock carries the messages of time, and the wonder of Creation. Lightning is a natural phenomenon that can be replicated with electronic equipment, yet, why would one want to do this? There is nothing like watching natural lightning. Snow is a wondrous experience, yet, we create machines that can replicate the experience.

I know of a wealthy individual who spent a small fortune renting a machine that could create artificial snow on the front yard of his Southern California estate. He did this for his two children. With all of his money, why didn't he just simply drive them (or have his chauffeur drive them) to the nearby mountains where they could experience real snow? Certainly it could not have been more expensive that renting ungainly machinery simply to recreate something that only nature can truly provide. Yet, that is the mentality that so many people end up having. They feel that they can create, or recreate, nature all around them.

One glance at the magazines of the rich and famous reveals the extent to which companies pander to this wish among the wealthy. There are companies that create waterfalls, boulders, jungly atmospheres, and other "natural" surroundings. Yet, as nice as they may be, they are poor substitutes for nature. Man has come to feel that he can replace God. Want a forest in your back yard? No problem, just whip out a few hundred thousand dollars, and you can have a forest. Want a waterfall in your front yard? Not a problem, it can be yours for roughly the same amount as the artificial forest in your backyard.

People work for, and strive to attain, a world that they can control. It is theirs, and theirs alone to enjoy. The rest of the world can take care of itself. Leave me *alone*. I want to be left to my lonesome. The actual landscape of many of the mansions only serves to reinforce just how alone so many of these people want to be. I have seen homes that have a very long driveway which extends a considerable distance to the steps leading to the front door of the estate. These homes resemble Fort Knox. Shrubbery and trees completely hide the view of the home. It's like a secret military compound, or like the safe houses that the CIA reportedly uses for housing their operatives. I wouldn't be surprised if the security devices in the front of these homes require a retinal scan in order to gain entry. They probably have privately owned satellites watching down over the perimeter of their homes, always watching to see if someone gets too close.

Perhaps that is what adds to the mystique of the rich and famous. It is their exclusivity, the fact that they are so far beyond the reach of the masses. They are physically out of reach, protected by military-grade software and hardware. *But we, as a society, have elevated them to this position.* The mystique is not created because they are hard to reach. This mystique is entirely our own creation. We, as a collective culture, have all come to some unspoken agreement that these unsociable individuals are special. They are given demigod status. The more out of reach they are, the more we want to seek them out. One need only think of the mystique surrounding J.D. Salinger.

We attach this social status not only to celebrities, but also to certain elite groups, such as certain secret societies, who represent the cream of American leadership. One good example is the Skulls at Yale University. Their meetings are held in secret. I'm still not sure why. What would happen if the Skulls, all very famous and powerful leaders who are either current students or graduates from Yale, suddenly announced that they were going to meet in a faculty lounge on the campus at Yale, or at an exclusive restaurant in New Haven? What would happen? Would their power or prestige be in jeopardy? Would a meeting out in the open, in the light of day, threaten their agenda? Would the current infrastructure in America be threatened by a meeting of the Skulls that everyone knew about? Would it threaten international relations? Would it cause an international conflict?

We give the Skulls their mystique because *they are secretive.* It gives elite societies like the Skulls a certain amount of mystery that we find appealing. Yet this only perpetuates the social values to which we so steadfastly adhere. We want to belong to a secret elite society or group such as the Skulls. Or, we long to have that mansion that can only be reached by a long, winding road. To belong to the regular class of ordinary Americans who work for a living and have to pay bills seems somehow undesirable. It's not exciting enough, or sexy enough. We want to drive a sports car, because somehow a sexy blonde companion will materialize in the passenger seat.

Yet, this is all an illusion. Even if a sexy person were to approach you as you drive a sports car, they may very well be attracted to the sports car, *not you.* And that's because they are also slaves to materialism. That's where the emptiness comes in. We all want to be loved, and not for what kind of vehicle we drive, but for whom we are. When we read about celebrities who end up on drugs, it may very well be because they wised up to the fact that the people around them (whom they thought were true friends) were only attracted to the material possessions and fame of the celebrities. Their new 'friends' stick around only because of the mansions, and the goodies and gadgets, not because they are authentic friends with the person who became a celebrity. And they certainly were not friends with these celebrities *before* they became famous, only after.

Thus, in wanting to be loved and to feel loved, they come to realize that the "love" they were receiving was nothing of the kind. It was freeloading from other materialistic individuals whose "love" was conditional upon the enjoyment of materialism or fame. And, as soon as the fame and money disappeared, so did the "friends." And this is why, I believe, so many of these celebrities end up on drugs or become alcoholics. They realize that they were never truly loved for who they are. The drugs and alcohol serve to numb this sobering realization. The emptiness they must feel as a result of not having a more centered lifestyle becomes more and more obvious.

As of this writing, the singer Whitney Houston was found dead in a hotel in Beverly Hills. It appears that Ms. Houston most likely took her own life. It had been rumored that she had been using drugs for some time. And, just a short time ago, the actress Demi Moore was said to have had a total breakdown. In both of these cases, it may seem that these women did not have the mental fortitude to face the fact that they were growing older. In a youth-centered society and culture such as we have, this may seem to be the inevitable result.

Yet, it doesn't have to be this way. Celebrities behave in this dramatic and childish manner when they cannot have their way anymore. They want their fame, and their money, and the adoring fans, and they want it *now*. It is a pattern of thought that is not much more evolved from a four-year old infant. And, when they cannot have what they want, they throw their royal tantrums. However, as opposed to the tantrums that a four-year-old can throw, the tantrums that celebrities throw are more dramatic. They show up dead with drugs in their veins, or end up as alcoholics.

Yet, no one seems to question why they have these meltdowns. I do. Not only do I question why celebrities have them, but I even dare to propose a possible reason behind the histrionics in Hollywood. These actresses, and the others who have also had their meltdowns, such as Lindsay Lohan, or Britney Spears, seem to represent a generation of individuals in Hollywood who become such slaves to the love and adoration of the fans that they lose their sanity when their popularity diminishes. They become too attached to the fame and money that the Hollywood lifestyle brings, and when they are no longer famous, or rich, they turn to drugs, or, suicide.

This, of course, is nothing new. One need only think of Elvis Presley or Marilyn Monroe. Yet, the press does nothing to allow us a moment of pause to wonder if there is something "not quite right" in this picture. After these celebrities die, the press publishes the glossy magazine tributes to these deposed demigods. Fans and relatives are interviewed on television. Yet, no one actually stops to wonder if there is something unhealthy about what is happening to these people. Yet, this ties in with the theme that will be woven throughout this book. So many of these celebrities have become mental slaves to their fame and fortune. This enslavement is, I believe, at the root of their eventual downfalls.

They have no other identity than the one they peddle on stage, or on screen, and it seems that no one has warned them that fame is a fleeting experience. Furthermore, this kind of crash is what can happen when people do not have any sort of belief system, or faith in a power greater than themselves. They become their own gods, at the center of their own universes. And, like a god, they also believe that they have rights and privileges over and above the ordinary individual. They are no longer average, working-class citizens. They are now Hollywood Celebrities, and, as such, they feel that they owe society nothing. On top of this, they take on an attitude of being more important than everyone else in society. Of course, the media and the press do little to help this situation. The press will take notice of every little detail about the lives of celebrities and magnify it to a ridiculous degree. A tattoo that a celebrity has (or where on her body it is situated), or a certain dress that a Hollywood starlet wore to the Academy Awards make front-page headlines. With the press giving them that level of attention, it's not hard to see why these celebrities crack up when they're no longer receiving that level of adulation.

The press, along with society, becomes the overindulgent parents, and the celebrities become the whiny, overindulged infants who cry, whine, and throw tantrums when they are not getting their way. Or worse, they take their own lives. It's enough to cause one to be thankful that one is not a celebrity! And, yet, becoming a celebrity with demigod status is exactly what so many people, particularly young people, seem to aspire to these days. This is how the system is perpetuated. Many people are not content with living a simple yet well-contented life. It seems that only celebrity stardom will do for many people. The reason for this is that our society has not changed its values. We still feel that celebrities, with all of their drugs, drama, and suicides, are still living a lifestyle that we would like to emulate. Nothing has changed. Hollywood still glamorizes the lifestyles of celebrities. Outside of Tinseltown, we still idolize famous athletes, moguls, and other famous individuals. It seems that no one wants to challenge the system because the attraction to the celebrity lifestyle is still much too attractive to us to give it up. Part of the reason for this may be found in the fact that all of us want to have role models, and people we can look up to in our lives for inspiration. Yet so few of us choose truly grounded people as our heroes, or choose people with simple lifestyles as our role models. And yet, this is what is necessary.

What is needed is a change in consciousness. Our society has to begin a process of questioning the values with which we are raised to see if they are still in our best interest to keep. Do we really want to idolize people who shoot drugs into their veins when they are not getting the fame they desire? Do we really want to idolize people who take their own lives when they feel depressed? Hopefully, this book can contribute in some small way to the start of an open-minded dialog in which these questions can be put to the fore.

Nevertheless, the values that are firmly in place in society are what help to keep people aspiring to materialistic lifestyles. No matter what the origin of the image, people want to live their lives like the celebrities they read about, and they will work themselves to the bone in order to attain that standard of living. I know a college professor of anthropology who, at the time I first met him, was working almost around the clock in order to afford the spacious house he and his family enjoyed. He once confided to me that he was teaching almost two full sets of college classes in order to earn the extra money he needed to pay for the lifestyle that he and his family wanted. The house they lived in was impressive. It was a two story home with a spacious backyard and a swimming pool.

Every year, this professor takes a group of students from his anthropology classes with him to a foreign country. These excursions provide these students with the opportunity to study cultures in "real world" settings, rather than just in the classroom. Both before and after the trip, he invites his students over to his spacious home and shows photo slides of the country they will be visiting, or photo slides of places which they had just visited. It provides a nice venue for his students to socialize, and his home did create a nice ambiance. Yet, his home and the lifestyle that he and his family had become accustomed to was becoming a source of stress for this gentleman. He was working tirelessly merely to afford a home that was larger than he needed it to be. This professor and his ex-wife had only two children. Yet, they felt that they needed the overly-developed home in which they lived, as well as all of the amenities within and without.

The capacious home, minivan, and swimming pool that they enjoyed are quite normal for our society. Scores of families live in homes equal in size or even larger. However, what may be a source of concern for some social critics, myself included, is that so many families confuse needs with luxuries. Countless Americans feel that they cannot live without a two-story home (with an attic), a large kitchen (with an island), and a recreation room with an extra-large flat screen plasma television (with Internet hookup) a two-car garage, and a swimming pool (with Jacuzzi). This has even become part of our national identity.

The massive economic recession which began in 2008 has caused many people to take stock of their lives. This may very well be the time when you can ask yourself some key questions, such as: Do I really need all of the material possessions that I have? Do I really need to be chasing after more material items that certain marketers are clever enough to make us believe that we "need?" You may be surprised by how little you really need in life. We have become so used to feeling that we need a lot of "stuff" in order to be happy in life.

The result of the recession of 2008 and beyond is that it caused many people in society to realize that money is not always going to be available. The jobs that we have, and the incomes that they produce, are not something that we can count on anymore. Many jobs disappeared in the recession, not the least of which was in education. The effect has been devastating. So many sectors of the national economy have been affected. This is akin to what happened to the aerospace corporations in the recession of the early 1990s. However, the scale of the damage now is much larger.

The modern American family still yearns for the two-story, three or four bedroom house (in a nice neighborhood, thank you very much), a flat-screen television, a laptop computer (in addition to the family computer in the den), CD players, an iPad, or an iPhone, Kindle Reader, and a Blu-ray player on which to watch movies. And, of course, there are always the upgrades. Nowadays, it is not enough to watch movies on a Blu-ray player, but to watch them in 3-D. The hunger for these things is still there. I suppose what I find most troubling about this phenomenon is that it is occurring during one of the most severe economic breakdowns in American history. Many people do not want to let go of the incessant desire for more. And, the ever-present credit companies can always be counted on to be the ones who are still hungrily attempting to lend money in order to make money. The system will stay in place as long as people feel that they must purchase something in order to be happy.

And yet, this is the very time in which you can liberate yourself. This is the time in which you, the reader, can decide that you no longer want to be a slave to the materialistic demands placed on us in society. You don't have to be like everyone else. The choice is in your hands to be different. There is an irony in society. American culture is said to be based on rugged individualism, and, to a very large extent, that is true. Yet, what I see from a sociological perspective is that fewer and fewer people in society seem to have the courage to be true individuals and declare that they do not want to keep up with the Joneses. It seems paradoxical that in a country based on individualism, there is a great tendency towards group think. There may be a clue as to why: anxiety.

Many people seem to harbor an anxiety that they will be questioned if they do not go along with society. There is a certain amount of truth to this. I have been questioned or given subtle (or not so subtle) comments which hint at others' disapproval that I don't possess the latest gadget, or car, or other such material commodity. The reality, or paradox, is that people might question anyone who doesn't give himself over, unquestioningly, to society's incessant materialistic fads. It can be very threatening to insecure people to suddenly be confronted by a grounded person who displays a healthy amount of free thinking.

However, corporate America does not want you to be a free thinking individual. And, perhaps most ironic of all, corporate America does not want you to be a rugged individual, someone who can safely dismiss their pleas for you to purchase their wares. It takes a fair amount of ego strength to be able to question the demands made on us. At times, those demands are made very openly. Only recently, it was heard here and there that in order to help the economy, that we should spend our money. Really? We need to spend money? On what? Things we don't need? Using the very credit that got us into the hole in the first place?

When the economy becomes slim, I certainly am not going to put others' financial solvency ahead of my own. If I don't need to spend, then I won't. And, if some of these businesses fail as a result of many people not purchasing their goods or services, then perhaps, as it is said in the realm of relationships, it was not meant to be. Perhaps the goods and services that do not survive were never really meant to have a long life in the economy, so what we see many only be the inevitable result of supply and demand. Yet, one has to be somewhat in awe of the candor of people telling us to spend.

It takes a lot of nerve to say that, not to mention a lot of self-centeredness. And, perhaps, it is encouraging that the message is out in society. Perhaps it signals an end to uncontrolled consumption. Now, the companies and corporations are starting to panic, and they give up their hue and cry for people to spend. Do not give in to the message to spend your hard-earned money on things that you don't really need. Even if companies are begging us to spend, we must resist this message. They are thinking only of their own benefit, which comes at the cost of our money, which is what they want. Corporate American companies are doing what they have done for two centuries: they are looking after their own bottom line. They need us to spend money on the goods and services that they produce. Yet, we, as citizens, are the ones with the power to resist that pressure. It is our right not to spend if we do not want to spend.

If an item, such as a sweater, or a new jacket, will truly make you happy, then by all means purchase the item. The critical difference is that the purchase does not come about as a result of corporate pressure to do our civic "duty" by spending money. The two are very different conditions. I have personally purchased some shirts and jackets that I genuinely like, and truly enjoy wearing them. And, of course, it feels good when people give me compliments. Yet, there is a crucial difference that I must point out. I purchased those items strictly for myself. I did not purchase them in order to keep up with the Joneses. If they just happen to be what the Joneses wear, that's fine. However, I couldn't care less what the Jonses wear. The reason is that I am not in a fashion competition with them. I wear only the clothes that make me happy. I have long let go of the need to satisfy other people's wishes to conform. The anxiety to conform that may have once been there is now long gone. Yet, I see many people still acting out of that anxiousness to be just like everyone else.

In order to begin the process of liberating yourself from this insidious effect from society, ask yourself some key questions. First of all, ask yourself what would happen if people didn't like the fact that you have a regular television, instead of a flat-screen plasma television. Or that you have an older computer? What would happen if they didn't like this about you? If any of your friends are making any sort of derogatory comments about your lifestyle based upon the fact that the technology in your home is not up to snuff, then perhaps they don't deserve your (or anyone else's) friendship. Honestly, if that is the sort of individuals who you have in your life, you may want to consider finding some new friends. Some of these behaviors that we see in adults may very well be a carryover from our childhoods. And, perhaps the pressure to conform is nowhere as dramatic as it is in childhood. Children feel a strong need to fit in, and be part of the "in-crowd." This is a result of very clever mental programming by corporate America. It is said that the programming to consume begins in the cradle and goes with us to the grave.

The reason that your friends would feel threatened by your becoming a freethinker is that it would force them to look at their own lives. It would cause them to look in the proverbial mirror and ask themselves some very difficult questions, such as: Have I also been a slave to the materialistic demands made upon me by society? Some people have a vested interest in having you think the way they do. It's easier to go along with the illusion than to face reality. And, the manner in which some people react to reality is very dramatic. I once watched a documentary about the negative consequences of credit, and it showed the mothers of two young people, both of whom took their lives when they realized that they could not afford to pay off an insurmountable debt owed on many credit cards. The story was very moving, and I was truly touched by it. What was so vivid was the candidness of the mothers who expressed their feelings so openly. However, as sad as I was while watching the documentary, I cannot say that I am the least bit surprised. Young adults in particular are vulnerable to the phenomenon of rampant misuse of credit. I believe I may know the reason why.

While in college, many young adults get their first "real" jobs and begin to earn "real" money. And, with a real paycheck in their pockets, they set about acquiring the things which they had been pining for, but, up until now, had been depending on their parents to purchase for them. It may very well be the case that those young adults whose parents were unable to buy them many things on birthdays or Christmas are going to the ones who will begin acquiring the most purchases. If you were to take a tour around any major university's parking lot, you would most likely find a host of brand new or luxury vehicles. The idea of monastic simplicity and cloistered asceticism as part of university life is lost on many of these young adults.

In previous generations, most young people went to college, lived simply (consuming much beer and pizza) and lived the monastic life that university life imposes. The fun would come in the form of fraternity or sorority parties, late-night hook-ups, and getting drunk after a difficult week. However, it was somehow understood that all of this privation would pay off one day, in the form of a high-paying job, or at least a career that would allow the average graduate to support a family. That was the reward of graduation. The beer and pizza would become a fond memory, only to be supplanted by fine wine and haute cuisine as new forms of culinary delight.

Life was seen as a series of normal stages, and the transition from one stage to the next was marked, and celebrated. Now, however, all of these stages have become blurred. Many modern students live with a domestic partner, in an apartment, drive brand-new cars, go to school part-time, and carry a significant amount of debt. I have spoken to students over the years who claim that they had to work long hours in order to pay off a car, or other major expense. Yet, these were not items that the student truly needed. They could have waited until they graduated from college. It was the mass-marketing ploy of credit card companies who made it possible for these students to enjoy instant gratification in the form of being able to drive off the lot in the new car, or out the store with a new laptop computer. Many students end up leaving college altogether in order to work longer hours, and attempt to pay off their debt. And, if you factor in student loan debt, the reality becomes even grimmer. This grim reality, however, is what is occurring in our society.

That is why I stand opposed to the idea of credit card companies appearing on college campuses and setting up their tables and targeting the very people who are least able to pay off debt. And, it seems counter intuitive. Why go to the colleges and universities to entice young people who have very little money to sign up for a credit card? Of course, the usual little sales gimmicks are utilized, such as free little stuffed animals, or Frisbees, or t-shirts to those who sign up for the card.

The other factor at work in the process of developing a resistance to group think is the development of our identity. This process normally occurs during the tumultuous period of our adolescence. We struggle to understand who we are, and what we value, and what we want out of life. This is also a period during which we are exploring our choices as to what kind of career we want to have as adults. And this can be a very difficult period, one of great adjustment and conflicting values and conflicting emotions. As we grow a little bit older and progress into the college years, this process begins to slow down and is not quite as dramatic as when we were in our early teen years.

Around the time that young people go to college, they begin to acquire a more solidified sense of who they are. Their identity has crystallized to the point where they begin to gain or form a general and vague sense of what they want out of life. The development of a person's identity is important and the reason I point this out is that many of the motivations that people feel to spend money are based upon their own wish to express their identity. Most of us have purchased things based upon our own impression of our own individual identity, for instance, certain types of clothes or a certain type of automobile, or make-up or shoes.

Yet, there is an irony here. So many of us want to have our own individual identity and don't want to be a clone of someone else. Many people have read the accounts of people who live in Communist countries where everyone is dressed the same and work the same. The impression that one gets from reading these stories is that these people are clones or robots, having been made in a factory, as it were. And, for many of us here in the West, that may not have much appeal at all because there is so much emphasis in our culture regarding the development of our individual identity. This is nothing new of course. Ever since the foundation of our Republic, the notion of rugged individualism has been the cornerstone of our American identity. One need only think of iconic images like the Marlborough Man, or the cowboy of the American West who represents the self-made man and rides off into the sunset, alone. Therefore, the concept of individuality and individualism is a traditional cornerstone of American identity. And yet, there is a curious phenomenon at work in our society. So many of us want to have an individual identity, but, what we see in our culture of consumption is that everyone ends up looking the same as everyone else, and no one seems to want be left behind.

It seems to be a kind of cultural irony or, one can even dare to categorize this behavior as cultural hypocrisy. While so many people want to be rugged individualists, it seems that everyone is running out to the stores to purchase what everyone else has. Ergo, the result is that everyone has the same type of car, or the same type of clothes, or the same type of iPhone, or some other modern widget. It seems that we have come to a point in our society were people, particularly young people, don't want to be left out of the in-crowd, so they rush out to purchase what everyone else is buying. One need only think of the phenomenon of the iPhone, or the Xbox video games. It seems like everyone has to have one of these items. And, this is a true contradiction because no one wants to be left out, yet everyone wants to be individualistic, yet, in essence, the two states are irreconcilable.

To dare to be different requires true courage because, in a society where there is such pressure from corporate America to purchase the same type of automobile, or the same type of clothing, and use the same type of computer. Anyone who decides not to subscribe to that consumerist mentality will be viewed as different, or will stand apart. He or she will be alone. Yet that is in essence the very core message of this book. I am challenging you, as the reader, to dare to be different. When I use the word "different" in this context, I am referring specifically to having the courage not to give into the pressures being placed upon us by corporate America. I am not referring to anyone not conforming in any other way. I am merely referring to willful resistance not to acquiesce to the materialistic lifestyle being promoted by corporate America. And, this pressure to conform, in a material sense, can be quite strong.

I remember that one of my first cars was a plain-looking old Dodge. One of my friends at that time suggested to me that I save up enough money so that I could purchase a more 'stylish' vehicle. And yet, his suggestion that I buy a more stylish car is a prime example of the kind of groupthink that I am daring readers not to give in to anymore. So many of us want to belong to the in-crowd and no one wants to be different. With respect to automobiles, it seems that so many people want to have or drive the newest or most stylish model. There are numerous examples of people leasing cars because they cannot even afford to purchase an automobile, merely so that they can have the appearance of driving a new vehicle.

In the community where I live, it seems as though the most important goal in life is to drive the latest or most luxurious automobile, such a Mercedes, or Audi, or a BMW. And it seems as though no matter what level of income, the most important thing is to be able to drive through the streets of Los Angeles and be considered a *somebody*. No one wants to be considered a *nobody* but the extent to which people go to appear to be a somebody can, and does, reach the level of ridiculous. Why would anyone want to collect welfare checks merely to lease a BMW? Clearly, some people don't have their priorities in the right order. The acquisition of luxury automobiles, when one is poor, is basically a form of falsehood and phoniness. It is a dishonest representation of one's self.

What's wrong with driving a modest Dodge, like the one I used to drive? Why does it have to be stylish? Why does it have to be a new car? Why does it have to be what everyone else is driving? Why should I spend my money to buy a car merely to satisfy other people's sense of aesthetics, particularly if impressing other people with a vehicle is not important to me? At this point in my life, when I think of automobiles, all I really consider is that I have a reliable means of transportation: a strong engine, good tires, and enough capacity to drive me to and from work, and other forms of discretionary driving. That's all I need.

I don't need to be driving a luxury automobile or something that is "stylish." Yet, so many people, who perhaps are less enlightened, or are more vulnerable to what others think of them, or who continuously need a sense of approbation from others, cave in to these societal pressures. They give in to the pressures around them to drive a certain type of automobile merely to have a certain kind of image. Having lived where I do for the past eleven years, it's been quite an education to witness the actions of people around me who feel that they must go to whatever lengths are necessary to acquire luxury vehicles, merely to project an outward image of status.

Why this is so important to them, is, at first blush, beyond me. However, in a general sense, and particularly from a psychological perspective, the more effort an individual exerts into projecting a certain kind of image that is not in conjunction with, or parallel to, reality, the more it may seem that the person or persons who are doing this are suffering from a personal or collective sense of inferiority. Only an inferiority complex could cause a person or a group of people, perhaps even an entire culture to overextend themselves, merely to project an image that is not accurate, honest, or real. If a person is suffering from an inferiority complex, what typically occurs is that the complex is turned inside out, and the person begins to overinflate or exaggerate their own sense of self-importance. A truly grounded, or healthy individual, is normally humble and not boastful.

However, only someone who feels inadequate or inferior goes to such lengths to impress other people or are boastful in one way or another. It is a linear relationship. In other words, there is a negative correlation at work. The greater the sense of inadequacy or inferiority, the greater the effort to overcompensate and impress everyone by means of showy gestures, such as driving new luxury automobile whilst living in Section 8 government subsidized housing, or popularly known as the "projects." These gyrations make up for an emptiness they feel inside, and I will be addressing this emptiness later in this book. Suffice it to say that only feelings of inferiority can cause someone to go to such great lengths to project a false and dishonest image of who they really are.

Nevertheless, what I see in the community where I live is a more exaggerated form of what is happening in our society in general. People expend great effort to acquire items, such as large homes or certain types of cars, in order to project a certain kind of image. The psychological commodity that people most likely want to project is status. They want to appear as if they are from a higher socioeconomic stratum in our society. People may drive certain automobiles, or wear certain designer-brand clothing or may even just carry themselves in a certain way so that they can pretend to be what they are truly not in reality. (Behavior is measured on a continuum, and this pretending, taken to an extreme form, is what can give rise to severe mental illness.)

One need only think of *The Great Gatsby* and the extent to which Jay Gatsby went to project an external image of success. In the story, the efforts that he put forth to create this image were extraordinary. Nevertheless, what I see in society is people clamoring to buy the latest iPhone or iPad, or computer or SUV, so that they can keep up with everyone else. It makes one think of the overused and trite expression that they are "keeping up with the Jonses." Yet, trite as this may sound, this is exactly what they are doing. They are trying to keep up with everyone else. However, what they are doing is working against them. As long as they continue to spend money for these reasons, their need to keep up with other people will end up being financially self-injurious to them. If people are buying watches, or clothes that they cannot afford, or leasing automobiles that they cannot afford, then that level of spending is self-destructive.

People are driving themselves to bankruptcy, literally, merely to project an image of themselves which is nothing more than a mirage in a desert of superficiality and falsehood. This is where the central dare in my book comes into focus. What would happen if you, as the reader, decided not to give in anymore to this cycle of spending merely to keep up with others? What if you decided not to give into society's pressure to purchase the latest computer or the latest vehicle on the market? After this recession began in 2008, I had to make some rather difficult decisions myself. Like so many others, I also admired clothing that looked nice or stylish, as well as the other niceties that are constantly being advertised in our society.

Yet, I had to realize that having those things is not worth jeopardizing my own financial well-being. I am not going to spend what money I have merely to project a phony image or to satisfy the moguls of corporate America. It takes a real act of courage and bold resistance not to give in on that level. You have to be true individualist not to give into that type of groupthink that seems to be what causes everyone to run out to purchase what everyone else has. In a sense, I consider myself to be more true to the rugged individualism upon which this nation was founded so long ago. Those who cave in and purchase what everyone else is buying have lost touch with the pioneering spirit.

Most people have been exposed to anti-Communist literature which describes how nobody is allowed to be different in a communist society. Everyone is supposed to look the same, and more or less dress the same, and have the same level of financial resources as everyone else. A Communist society is supposed to have all of the proletariat looking like they were mass produced in the very factories in which they make their living. Those of us, like me, who were given strong anti-Communistic propaganda in school, ended up believing that such as life was bland, or lacked color. How boring if everyone is the same! The same kind of car, the same type of Chairman Mao-type uniforms, such as the ones they wear in China.

We viewed Communist society as a land of zombies all moving in slow motion because there is little incentive to work hard because the state ends up taking people's earnings and all that's left is a wish to defect to the West. That's what they told me life was like in a Communist society. It was presented like Purgatory, or like living Limbo. It was not Heaven, but it was not really Hell either. It was somewhere between those two empires. What that type of indoctrination is supposed to do is to turn young people off of socialism and communism by presenting them as forms of statism where everyone is the same, and that is supposed to be bad. There are no rich people, and no poor people. Just the working class, who own their means of production. But the net result is a strong distaste in students for the concept "sameness."

The thought of everyone looking the same and acting the same is presented as boring, unexciting. Yet, what we have is almost its corollary. We have a free society based upon capitalism. Within this system, we have people all clamoring to buy the same types of cars, the same types of clothes, and the same types of phones and computers. And what is the result of all this? Everyone is the same. Everyone is striving for the two-story home with the pool in the backyard and the two cars, and the white picket fence, in other words, the American Dream. But what has happened is that we have a society where there is more "sameness" than people care to admit to, or accede.

A drive across large tracts of land between Los Angeles and San Diego reveals tract housing, also known as mushroom communities. The houses all look exactly the same. The cars in the driveways look more or less the same. Even the manicured lawns and the trees planted in the front yard all look the same. Moreover, the residents in these areas shop at malls that also have the same stores that you find everywhere else: Walmart, Kmart, Barnes & Noble, Chase Bank, Best Buy, Toys R Us, Ralphs, Vons, and Jiffy Lube. These little communities are replicated *ad infinitum* all across America. They all look the same. You could parachute down to the middle of Orange County, California and then drop down in the middle of Prince George's County, Maryland. You probably wouldn't be able to spot the difference. Yet, we pride ourselves in not living in a Communist or Socialist society where everyone is the same. There is a disparity between the political rhetoric that we hear and the reality of our society.

We have entire cities that are clones of each other. The residents of the tract housing communities all leave their mass-produced homes at 8:00am, drive to work in their mass-produced vehicles, crowd the same freeways, and, at 5:00pm all come driving home on the same congested freeways to their homes and relax in their mass-produced Jacuzzis and swimming pools. Thank God we're not Communists! However, I am able to see behind the rhetoric to see what is truly at work. As children, we are told that Communism, or any form of statism is bad, and that we are truly blessed to live in a free society. And, we are truly blessed in many ways. I don't deny this in any form. But, the purpose of the anti-Communist rhetoric is to raise new generations of consumers who will not rock the capitalistic boat that we use to sail in financial waters. By drilling into our heads that Communism and Socialism are bad, the free enterprise system is maintained, and remains free of any threat to its existence.

This is what is happening on the other end of the political spectrum. It is well known that people in Russia were told horror stories about life in the West to keep them from defecting, or jumping over the Berlin Wall. The Russian state had a vested interest in keeping people from wanting to come to America. Every social system must maintain itself alive by making people believe that what they have is better than any other form of government or financial system. Therefore, it is of little surprise to me that I was given very explicit anti-Communist messages while I was in school. My teachers felt it was their moral obligation to teach us children that capitalism is good so that one day we could do our civic duty by spending our hard-earned money.

In order to maintain people believing that our capitalistic and free-enterprise system is the best in the world, which many do, it is imperative that the programming start when students are young. This way they will not become revolutionaries and overthrow the system. There are very wealthy corporate moguls whose financial empires can only be sustained by having our citizenry continue to believe that capitalism is good and that Communism is bad. Their financial survival depends on it. They certainly have a vested interest in having teachers and parents teach their young charges that life is great in our society and that life in Communist societies is miserable. Even Hollywood movies like *Moscow on the Hudson* strove to present life in the Soviet Union as miserable. It is not surprising that even movies are used as political tools to further the indoctrination in our society.

Every form of communication is in service of the capitalist system: the messages we receive, the literature we read, and the rhetoric we are exposed to on a daily basis. Ultimately, the only reliable source of information that we can have are the first-hand reports of people who have lived in both types of society. I have known a few people who have lived in both types of societies and the reports are mixed at best. However, I wish to point out that this book is not attempting to endorse one form of political or economic system over another one. The purpose of this book is merely to raise some very important and pertinent rhetorical questions. Hopefully, by raising these questions in rhetorical form, it can stimulate much needed discourse, and empower citizens to make more informed decisions about their money and spending habits.

It takes a considerable amount of strength to buck these forces and to stand apart from the economic entrapment that is so prevalent in our society. However, one does not need to be a revolutionary. There is no need to overthrow the system. It seems to make many people perfectly happy, and, if it works for them, more power to them. I merely wish to stand apart. Not above, merely apart. I do not wish to partake of the system. It does not make me happy, so I choose not to be another debt-ridden participant. I have been driving cars that are neither stylish nor new. I have shirts that are over a decade old. And yet, that brings me back to my primary question in this book: what would happen if you were to choose not to give into the kind of corporate pressure that is being shoved toward us from womb to tomb?

What would happen if you were to drive an older car? Are you afraid of what others would think of you? Better yet, what would happen if you took the bus to work? Do you think that people would mock your lifestyle? What would happen if you did not wear the latest or most fashionable clothing? These are the kinds of questions that readers must ask themselves and I do not presume to have all the answers to these questions. My role is merely that of a social critic, or in Wilhelm Reich's terminology, a *cultural philosopher*. These are weighty matters to be sure. Countless families have had to cut back on unnecessary expenditures or niceties that are no longer considered essential. Therefore, it is in the midst of the economic turmoil in which we find ourselves that I ask these very relevant questions.

However, it seems that so many of us in our society, particularly young people, feel uncomfortable with the idea that they will not be part of the in-crowd. And yet, one can be part of the in-crowd without necessarily having to purchase the in-crowd accoutrements. If a young person wishes to associate with a group of friends, that youngster may very well find herself being pressured to spend money that she doesn't really have. That is when they begin to beg their parents for a credit card. However, young people have to ask themselves whether they really want to associate with others their age who will judge them based upon the car they drive or the clothes they wear. Unfortunately, in order to gain a sense of entre into the hip crowd, countless young people go out and buy the clothes, music, or cars that their friends are driving.

There is nothing inherently wrong with wanting to have a group of friends or a supportive social network. But true friends will value you for you who are, not the kind of vehicle you drive, or the type of shoes you wear. However, what is truly sad is that so many young people grow up into adulthood with exactly *the same mentality*. They grow up and see other soccer mom and dads driving a certain type of SUV, which causes them to feel that they must also buy a similar SUV (or better yet, one that is larger!). Or, they must keep up with their friends and put a down payment on a home that is comparable in size with the houses in which their friends are living. It's a mentality that begins in early childhood and does not end until we pass on.

I am not sure what it will take to cause more people to turn to a more sensible form of living. Perhaps the recession that we are facing will have to become worse in order for people to feel that it might be in their best interest to abdicate the incessant need to purchase the latest item that is being advertised by corporate America. In essence, I see this recession as having created two groups of people: one group of people will be those who have learned their lesson of over-consumption and have reformed themselves. They will now consider the benefits of having a carefully crafted budget and sticking to that budget. The second group of people will be the ones who merely cut back on their spending temporarily, only to take it up again once the financial storm has passed and the economic skies are once again clear. All it will take is a new job, or a raise in pay, and they will return to their customary (pre-recession) levels of spending.

In essence, they haven't really changed, they just have cut back on their spending as a matter of course. I would like to believe that I am in the first group. I also had to learn some rough financial lessons regarding the dangers of reliance on credit and the important need for keeping and maintaining a budget. I do not pretend to have been born with this knowledge. I also had to rid myself of the wish to have certain materialistic niceties which I felt would make me happy. These were very difficult "real world" lessons that I had to learn. Yet, this is the type of learning that leads to real growth. And, in a sense, what this book is hoping to promote is growth in the reader.

My sincerest hope is that in reading this book, readers will, with time, grow and mature beyond their need to acquire material goods. Yet, one has to consider the fact that in changing one's lifestyle, one will encounter strong social forces. One need only drive along a freeway in any state and one will see a constant barrage of billboards advertising things: food establishments, or a set of stores, or shopping mall, or a new automobile. But there is a constant stream of advertisements that we are bombarded with on a daily basis goading us to go spend money on a good or service. Our entire economic system and way of life was built around this corporate mentality. In a sense, this is what allowed the United States to become the greatest economic empire in the world. The great barons of the 19th century created the enormous wealth that this country has enjoyed.

One need only think of financial giants such as J.P. Morgan or the Rockefeller family. The accomplishments that were achieved by these financial giants were truly meritorious and they deserve their place in the historical Hall of Fame. I am no less an admirer of those that created these financial empires. The mansions all along the coast of Long Island are a silent testament to the financial acumen and ingenuity which these economic geniuses demonstrated. I admire the fact that they were so industrious and hard-working. It takes an inordinate amount of ambition, hard work and industriousness to create a financial empire at the level of J.P. Morgan, for example. So it is not that I am not aware of the extraordinary talents of these individuals.

These were people whose intelligence, work ethic and dedication to building an empire should be admired and they should be given credit for what they accomplished. I have always been an admirer of the pioneering barons who were able to create a financial empire from very humble beginnings. So many of them hailed from poor immigrant families and as soon as their ancestors settled in the United States, they set about creating their wealth. On some level, I have even come to feel that the current economic turmoil which we are faced with calls for more individualists such as those barons to stimulate new financial creativity which might allow our economy to rebound from this deep economic conundrum in which we find ourselves.

Nevertheless what those early financial moguls did was to create an entire culture based on selling and buying. They established an entire economic system of consumption. Within this system people sell products or services and they go to great lengths to advertise their wares with great zeal, and appeals to people's emotions are made in order to get consumers to buy these items or services. Henry Ford was another such individual who devised a product that created mass appeal. The automobile became a classic icon of American individualism. People would no longer have to rely on public forms of transportation to get from one place to another.

There is an emotional attractiveness to the notion of independence and instant mobility. It appealed to people's sense of individualism and independence. There were others who, like Mr. Ford, developed other goods, such as household appliances. They likewise enjoyed great success because of the appeal to people's emotions. Yet, the momentum that this foundation began developed a velocity of its own and became an almost unstoppable force in our society, such that, for the last two hundred years, there has been an ever growing system based upon supply and demand, and consumerist appetites being sated by an endless variety of goods and services. Our society is based upon buying and selling. Businesses are built upon a product or service that is deemed to be of value and advertised in such a way as to create mass market appeal. We, as consumers, are then seduced into buying these goods or services.

One example of this is the usage of scantily clad models being used to advertise sports cars. And, hard as the buyer of said car may look for her, he will not find her anywhere in the automobile which he just purchased. But this is how corporate advertising works. They use things like sex appeal in order to get men and women to buy a certain product, as if the person in the commercial will magically appear with the product, like a genie. Perhaps this phenomenon would not be of as great interest to me as it currently is were it not for the fact that this level of consumerist mentality has reached a fever pitch and has developed an almost obsessive-compulsive quality to it.

It seems that there is nothing but an uninterrupted stream of images, ads, posters, billboards, sound bites, all pressuring us to buy something that, in all likelihood, we really don't need. Do we really need another automobile? Do we really need another computer? Do we really need another cell phone that has more apps than we know what to do with? Do we need more ways to read books electronically, rather than on the printed page? Do we need another guest bedroom in our future home? How much space do we need in order to feel that we have "privacy"? We have to ask ourselves: how much of these items do we really need? I knew a married couple, which, at one point, owned five automobiles. Do people really need five vehicles in order to feel happy? Do people really need that much in order to feel complete? These are the kinds of questions that this book will raise repeatedly in order to stimulate thought and discussion. We have to ask ourselves: when will it feel like we finally have enough "things" in our possession in order to feel fulfilled or sated.

There are other forms of satiety that people normally recognize. For example, when we sit down to eat a meal and become full, we normally push the plate away or stop eating because we have reached a level of satiety and at that point we can no longer accommodate more food. Otherwise, we become sick to our stomachs. Most of us know that it is unhealthy to consume too much food, particularly if it is fatty or greasy. It leads to undesirable consequences, such as weight gain. Over time, this pattern of consumption and the weight it causes people to gain can raise the chances of getting other life-threatening diseases, such as atherosclerosis, cancer, and diabetes. Thus, we are able to recognize the dangers of consuming too much fat, and the hazards of gaining too much weight.

Yet, as opposed to this culture of dietary caution, there seems to be a dearth of awareness or discussion in the media regarding the economic dangers of spending too much money and the hazards of living on credit. The dangers of eating an unhealthy diet are all too clear for everyone. Yet, it seems that no one is nearly as concerned about their "diet" or consumption of *material* goods. While it is true that piling up credit card debt doesn't have the potential to shorten your lifespan as does a fatty diet, it certainly will lead to a life of financial misery and hardship if it is not brought under control. Ironically, stress and hardship could have the potential to shorten your lifespan. Stress taxes the body, particularly the immune and cardiovascular systems. And, as I mentioned in an earlier section of this book, there have been people who have committed suicide as a result of insurmountable credit card debt. Thus, for them it most certainly did become a matter of life and death, as it did for their families.

My hope is that readers and consumers who read this book will begin to take back some of the power (and some of the money) that they have acquiesced to corporate America. We must empower ourselves to resist the pressure to spend money. And we must resist the pressures from our fellow consumers who also pressure us into buying the latest widget that is being mass-marketed. If our friends and acquaintances are questioning our choice to save our money, then we must ask ourselves whether these friendships are worth preserving.

A true friend should be able to look beyond his or her biases or preferences, and support you in a decision if it feels right for you. In the end, what matters most is that we be valued by who we are inside, rather than by the kind of car we drive or the size of our home. I would hope that this is what enlightened people ultimately want. That is, in the end, the only way that we can value an individual. Just because someone may live in a modest apartment or drives a modest car, or both, does not mean that that person is worth any less respect or consideration in our society. Yet, sadly, that is what happens in our society.

We feel that someone who drives a luxury sport car is more of an individual, or a more important person. Of course, this social bias is nothing new and has its roots in the human tendency toward biases and prejudices. Most of us know about other forms of discrimination, such as showing a preference to someone who is white, or male. Yet there are other types of prejudice as well, such as educational and economic prejudice. It seems that when people run out to buy the latest car, or to build the biggest home, one impression is that they may be attempting to avoid economic prejudice. They don't want to be the victims of this economic prejudice. They are afraid that others will look down on them if they appear to be part of the working class.

Yet, materialistic prejudice is exactly that — we are "pre-judging" someone based upon their material exterior. Of course, I am not referring to the more drastic examples, such as someone who dresses like a hobo or bum, and doesn't bathe or shave. Most of us would find that appearance unattractive, or off-putting. Hopefully, such an individual would evoke feelings of sympathy or charity among the well-heeled. However, this is not what I am referring to in this case. I am referring to someone who demonstrates more politeness to someone who rolls into a restaurant in a new Jaguar, rather than the next customer who rolls into the parking lot driving a used Toyota. We see this in children. So many are teased and harassed at school by the other kids because they are not wearing the "right" type of sneakers, or because they have the effrontery not to be wearing the "right" kind of logo on their shirts.

When I was 14 years old, one of my classmates seemed annoyed or offended because I happened to be enjoying the music of Simon and Garfunkel. Obviously, to this student, I was clearly listening to the "wrong" type of music. Who knew! I didn't realize that there is the right type of music to listen to and the wrong type of music to enjoy. Perhaps I would have been able to see his point if I had been listening to rap or heavy metal music, with gratuitous four-letter-words, and messages of violence. To this day, I find that kind of music to be of very poor taste, degrading to women, and an endorsement of a violent lifestyle. It seems that the more bullet holes a rapper show his fans, like the Stigmata, the more they look up to him, and I find that notion quite unsettling. It's difficult enough to find suitable role models for young students, particularly those of color. Then we find them worshiping rappers and the situation becomes worse.

Yet, with regard to my own dislike of music that endorses violence, there are studies linking rap music to a host of behavioral problems. Thus, there is a solid reason for my dislike of rap music. And yet, to this day, I have continued to enjoy the music of Simon and Garfunkel, and I have yet to hear anything degrading or offensive in their beautiful and poetic lyrics. And, to this day, at least to my knowledge, there has not been a single study published linking the lyrics of Simon and Garfunkel to behavioral problems in adolescents. Yet, to my classmate, there was something in the music of Simon and Garfunkel to be avoided at all cost, but, to this day, I have no idea what that was, or is.

Those types of harassing messages are very common among adolescents. They feel that they can decide for everyone else what type of clothing should be worn, and what type of music is acceptable. They might as well publish official lists of approved clothing, shoes, watches, cell phones, and music, and correspondingly, the music and clothing that are met with disapproval. Yet, what I find disturbing is that adolescents almost become the bullhorns for the corporate moguls on Main Street. It is as though corporate America has managed to brainwash adolescents to such an extent that these youngsters become their official ambassadors, and they are here to evangelize everyone and spread the gospel of capitalism. And, clearly, corporate America is pandering to this crowd.

Any look at the movie industry can see that the current panoply of movies being financed by the big movie studios is clearly aimed at an increasingly younger audience. Most movies now involve protagonists that are rarely older than 20. The *Harry Potter* books and movies only served to crystallize this movement. And, many of these movies are based upon young adult novels, such as *Hunger Games*. I am not quite sure where these adolescents are getting their money, but they are clearly spending it on these books and on these movies, and the publishing companies and the movie studios are having a wonderful time catering to these youngsters whose money is burning holes in their pockets. The entire industry is now slanted toward this young audience.

Part of the reason is that those over 30 begin to be more selective with the type of things they purchase, at least some of the time. They may not be as apt to buy young adult novels that are later turned into motion pictures. Those over 40 spend even less money, or spend it only on big ticket items, such as homes or cars. Those over 50 spend even less, as they are beginning to plan for an ultimate retirement. Those over 60 are going to spend even less money, and so on, and so forth. Therefore, the proverbial goose that lays golden eggs is somewhere between 12 and 18 years of age, metaphorically speaking. That's where the spending is taking place. Yet, this is unfortunate on two levels: no one is teaching young people to save their money, and they are clearly not learning this on their own. Secondly, the harassment that students inflict upon their fellow students merely because of their shoes or shirts are hurtful, disturbing, and can leave scars.

Countless parents are working long, difficult hours at their jobs and doing everything within their power to provide for their children. And, sometimes, a pair of sneakers from Payless Shoes is all these working class parents can afford, and many parents cannot afford even that. Many families shop at Goodwill and Salvation Army stores, and buy all their clothes second hand. But the teasing and taunting that the children of these parents receive at school is truly unfair. It is entirely possible that this teasing and taunting leaves small but distinct psychological wounds and these children grow up to be adults who find ways to compensate for these childhood experiences. These adults not only become very greedy and acquisitive, but also very snobby and make it a point to have the "right" kind of house in the "right" kind of neighborhood, and drive the "right" kind of vehicle.

All this effort in the adult years may very well be gratuitous overcompensation for the privation these adults experienced in their youth. They may very well be saying to themselves: "No one is going to tease or criticize me again. Furthermore, I will have all the right things, and people will envy me!" Yet, no one seems to notice that all of this childhood criticism from classmates serves to keep the system going. It keeps our capitalistic boat afloat and without any kind of rocking from revolutionaries. The childhood hurt, and the subsequent wish to grow up and "show them" by having the right car, or the right house, is all part of the big machine, and it serves to keep the gears turning slowly and steadily.

Every new generation is exposed to the same messages from their school peers, and then they grow up to buy the goods they couldn't afford as adolescents. And on and on it goes. Truthfully, it is a very impressive system. One cannot help but admire just how watertight it truly has become. It has virtually no holes in it. It is like a very well-designed luxury cruise liner, large and imposing, and, unlike, the Titanic, it seems that this machine is truly unstoppable and unsinkable. There are two hundred years of momentum behind this big boat, and no one is complaining about its very presence. On the contrary, it seems to always be able to find a welcome port in our society at virtually all levels.

It seems that there is an unspoken code in our society. The code implies that the older we get, the more we should own. As we enter our 30s and 40s and 50s we should have more and more to show for our efforts or our years of working, such as large home, or a fancy car, or timeshares in other countries. On some level, that seems to be equated to 'progress.' If a person is in his 40s or his 50s and still driving an economy car, or has a modest home, the unspoken message that society would like us to believe is that he has not progressed as much as he should have by this point in his life. Or, put another way, he has not demonstrated the level of ambition or industriousness that is expected of him. There probably are a lot of people who make these kinds of judgments. And yet, what does it matter if someone is in his 50s or 60s and still rents an apartment or rides the bus to work. That person probably has more saved up in his bank accounts than the more showy individuals who love to show off their possessions, but are quietly miserable because of the debt that they hide from everyone.

I once had a girlfriend who introduced me to one of her friends. This friend was in her 50s. We were both invited to this friend's apartment to visit. I found the apartment capacious and charmingly well-appointed. It was clean, had nice furnishings and the woman who lived in it seemed perfectly happy with life. Later that night, my girlfriend made a comment that I never forgot. She said what a pity it was that her friend, then in her 50s, was still renting and did not own property. I found the comment judgmental and terribly unfair, and I told her as much. I felt that she was making a negative judgment based on her (my girlfriend's) economic prejudices and society's prejudices.

What did it matter that her friend didn't own property? She seemed to be a perfectly contented woman, one who had traveled and loved and lived. Besides she continued to work and to pay her rent and was completely self-sufficient. She was not living off of welfare checks or free-loading from anyone. She was thoroughly self-sufficient. I was irate at my girlfriend for that comment and yet, I soon realized that it was not just my girlfriend who feels this way. It is a very common notion; you 'should' buy your own home by a certain age, or, you 'should' own property at a certain point in time.

I once was reading a self-help book which describes the "tyranny of the shoulds," in other words, the tyrannical effect that the social and psychological of "shoulds" have upon the human mind. I should go to the gym. I should go to visit my parents. I should contribute more to charity. I should go to church more often. Most of us internalize the messages that we hear from our parents, our teachers, and society at large, and then we replay these messages to ourselves all the time. It's as if we all have internal tape recorders in our heads and we continuously hit the Rewind button and replay the messages over and over. The messages become so ingrained and so automatic that we hardly question them anymore. That is the troublesome part. These messages from our parents and society (of course, our parents are usually echoing the messages of our society) are not given enough scrutiny in order to evaluate whether these messages, proscriptions, and prescriptions are worth following. There are some people who are happy not going to church, and there are others who find great happiness in going to the gym on a daily basis. The important thing is that everyone takes the time to evaluate whether the messages we received as children or adolescents have much merit. Many of them don't.

I know of one physician who told me that he takes a vitamin/mineral supplement regularly, and, because of that, he can eat whatever he wants! I was struck by how liberating that sounds. I seriously doubt whether this man eats steak and fudge every day, otherwise, he would be a lot larger. And, he rarely exercises. He told me that he and his wife go on walks about once a month. This image is hardly congruent with what we are told on a daily basis that we should do: eat three to five servings of fruits and vegetables, and to devote a few days a week for some form of cardiovascular exercise.

And yet, I was struck by how happy he appears, as well as vibrant and healthy. It may not be due to his vitamin supplements, but, rather, his vitality and youthfulness come from the fact that he loves his work, has no plans to retire, and has what appears to be a felicitous marriage. However, my overriding point is that he did not feel tethered to all of the rules of health that all of us are supposed to or "should" obey. It can be an enormously liberating feeling to have the courage to let go of the rules we grew up with, all the while maintaining a responsible lifestyle, working, paying your bills, paying your taxes, following laws, and respecting other people's rights (all of which should go without saying).

When I refer to "breaking the rules" I am merely referring to those part of our lives which don't impinge upon society, such as our dietary choices, or the clothes we wear, or how we spend our money or our time, particularly our free time on our own. Perhaps it might be fun to experiment by breaking some of your childhood rules. Why not have dessert first? Why not stay up late watching old scary movies from the 1950s? Why not decline a family dinner? Why not have a day of complete indulgence, including watching television, or reading a favorite book (for the fourth time) and eating bon bons all day? Why not go out and get a tattoo? As long as you're not going to drive a vehicle, why not get a little tipsy? Go ahead and skip bathing on a Saturday, or whatever day you don't go to work. Do it! *Dare to be different*. But this is where the trouble lies. There is double speak at work. Let me explain further.

I once saw a poster for Apple computers many years ago. The message at the bottom read: "Think different." Obviously the makers of Apple computers don't want you to think anything too "different" about the merits of Apple computers, or their supposed superiority over PCs, otherwise, no one would buy Apple products and they might lose money or go entirely out of business. Therefore, the makers of Apple computers want you to think different, but not in a way that might endanger their economic strength. On the contrary, they might very well want you to think "differently" about PCs, in other words, to form a negative impression about them, and to perhaps make a switch over to Apple computers. Go ahead and think different, but not *too different*. The message was vague. It had only two words: think different. One could question the ad and ask: think different about what? Computers? Society? About myself?

But, in the end, there is a disconnect between the messages we hear and the reality of our society. Think different, but not in a way that disrupts our economic and capitalistic system. Because when all is said and done, our society does not want anyone to think too different about capitalism. It becomes a threat to the system. There will be those who actually have the gall to come out and tell people to spend money. You have to admire their transparency. For example, I recently heard that our elected leaders were encouraging citizens to go out and spend money in order to stimulate the economy. What nerve! Many working class people don't have money to spend on discretionary items.

It reminds me of the movie *Jaws* when the mayor of Amityville was encouraging people to go into the water, merely to make the town and beach appear normal after a shark attack. Yet, the people knew that there was a large and dangerous shark wandering off the coast. But, rather than be concerned about people's physical safety, all he was worried about was the economic success of the town. He had the nerve (and stupidity) to tell the understandably frightened bathers to swim in the water (how having people swim in the ocean actually equates to economic success for a town is beyond me, but I am sure you understand the point being made here). Therefore, we are confronted with conflicting messages. Do we think differently, or not? In the end, society would rather have you conform to the system. Don't rock the boat or it could capsize! But the true question is: would we drown? I don't believe that we would.

I wonder what would happen if no one obeyed the mandate to go out and spend money. What would happen? A cascade of events would probably occur in a domino effect. There is no doubt that many businesses would suffer. Many retail outlets and franchises would close down. Yet, the remedy for that scenario is that the people who would lose their jobs could be absorbed into other areas of the economy that continue to function. Our society needs more adult education centers where laid off employees and business owners can go back to school. But rather than go back to college to learn about Medieval Europe, they can learn more ordinary skills that can be put to immediate usage into our economic system.

In a sense, what is need is a system of education that can admit people from the retail or service jobs that shut down in a bad recession, and then re-educate them to be able to work in a different sector of the economy all together. Perhaps some other people might need to go to a more traditional college. For example, if someone gets laid off and later decides that he or she wants to go to law school, then a more traditional system of schooling in our universities will be necessary. But it is foolish to tell working class people to go out and spend money. Why should they go into further debt merely to help someone else grow rich?

In a very bad recession a form of 'economic Darwinism' becomes the law of the land: survival of the fittest. If I have only a few hundred dollars in the bank, I am not going to spend them on products or services that I don't need. And no matter how patriotic I may be, I am not going to listen to elected leaders who command me (and others) to go and spend that money for the "greater good" of the economy. At that point, my own economic survival will be my priority. If Reebok goes out of business, my heart will go out to them, but I am not here to support Reebok.

I am not responsible for the economic solvency of any business. I patronize whom I choose, but only because I want to, not because some politician tells me to do so. We pride ourselves in not living in a Socialist or Communist system where the government tells you what to do, but, if our leaders are telling poor and working class people that they need to go and spend money, then our system of government is beginning to sound a lot like the statist governments people love to criticize. Again, double speak at work. If we are to live in a truly free and democratic society, then our leaders have to stop telling us what to do with our money.

In the final analysis, none of what people think of our material possessions matters at all. When you are on your deathbed, what will it have mattered what people thought of your home or your vehicle? Will it matter at that point? What will it matter that you did not have the latest in flat-screen plasma television technology? Will it be remembered at that point? You may want to consider this from the point of view of that moment, which we all will experience, when we are about to make the Great Transition, or pass way. It is fair to say that none of these petty matters will be on your mind at that point.

Would it not be infinitely better to look back with satisfaction that we served our fellow man? Would it not be better that we look back and feel proud that we made a small (or great) contribution to make the planet a more hospitable place? Or that we touched someone's life, and helped someone become actualized or helped someone feel loved. The only thing that matters at that point is what we gave of ourselves, not what we acquired. What also will matter is how much of our time and devotion we gave to help other people. Of course, there are the usual over-used expressions, such as "You can't take it with you," but there is truth to this.

We cannot take our possessions with us when we pass on to the next life. It is very difficult to accommodate a mansion into a coffin, and there are very few funeral homes that are willing to make a special coffin large enough for a Mercedes Benz. Yet that is how so many people think and behave. They become so attached to their homes and possession, and they lose sight of what's important. I remember so many times that I watched the news and saw a family that managed to escape a ravaging fire that destroyed their nice suburban home. It was a pity to see that, but, the most important thing is that they were able to escape with their lives.

A house can be replaced, but a human being cannot be replaced. Yet, when they would interview these people, they would be wailing, crying uncontrollably about the loss of their home. I do not mean to take anything away from their experience, or to sound callous. I am sure that being barely able to escape from a fire alive must be a horrible experience. However, what struck me about these people is the amount of grief they felt over the loss of their homes. It's a house. With the right type of home owner's fire insurance, it can be rebuilt. But you would think that they had lost someone, or watched someone die in the fire. Heavens!

Yet, in the end, I can hardly be surprised. People become so attached to their homes and their cars, and all of their possessions. To have a large home is part of the American Dream. It's what countless people strive for and dream about. But I never could get over my incredulity at seeing people's reactions while watching their home burn. A truly unfortunate experience, to be sure, but not one that would warrant such fever pitch grief! Their histrionics speak volumes about the values in our society. I have seen people more composed at funerals than while watching their homes burn.

A sense of scale is what is needed for so many people. People need to remember that very few things will matter in the end. God put us on this Earth to serve, not to acquire. I am not advocating that people leave all of their possessions and begin to live an ascetic life, like monks or nuns. Not at all. I am merely stating my belief that our purpose here is to make the Earth a better place. We are here to help others. We have to think about the next few generations that will come after us and the type of planet they will inherit. We are the stewards of planet Earth. God gave us this responsibility. Like the old expression, do you want to be part of the problem or part of the solution?

My sincerest hope is that current and future readers of this book will want to be the ones who engineer solutions to the pressing problems of our day, like finding cures for cancer, and finding ways of slowing down the destruction of the Earth's natural resources, or being able to forge better alliances with other countries, rather than a continuance of war. These are the subjects that matter, not whether your car is stylish enough to satisfy the fashion police in society. Life is about service, stewardship and fellowship. There are many ways in which this can be expressed. One can volunteer hours to tutor a student, or to plant a tree, or volunteer time for a beach clean-up. And, while engaged in those activities, one can meet other like-minded people, and those are the friendships that matter. Those are the friendships that have real, deep value, and are not sabotaged by pettiness or judgments.

I volunteered one Saturday at a local food processing facility. Volunteers that come in to this facility and they pack food and ship it to local soup kitchens and other distribution centers, so that poor, homeless, or needy people can have free food. It was enormously rewarding. It was gratifying to see people there from all walks of life, and at all age levels. The people who volunteer at these places are mature (key word?) enough to look beyond themselves, and are able to see the benefit of helping others. This is a quality that I see in short supply among so many in our society, particularly among those of younger generations. They still seem too wrapped up in themselves to see beyond their own material gratification.

Someone could come up with the counterargument and state that young people are normally self-absorbed, or self-centered. Furthermore, it could be said that the ability to see beyond one's self comes with age and maturity. This is true. Young people normally are self-absorbed. I was no different. Therefore, I am not concerned with young people and adolescents being self-centered. I am the first to admit that this is a normal element of that age range. However, the distinction I am trying to make is not that young people are selfish. That is to be expected. Rather, it is the insatiable need for young people to acquire material possessions. It seems to have taken on a life of its own. In previous generations, teenagers were more involved with who was dating who, or who was in love with whom, as well as deciding which college to attend, or what career was the right choice. The concerns of adolescents had more to do with people, and relationships, rather than material items.

Nowadays, I am sure that the teenage gossip of who's in love with who is still at work, but now, it also involves who has the latest iPhone, iPad, video games, designer-brand clothes and luxury automobiles. I am always amazed when I drive by the two local high schools in the city where I live. Seventeen-year-olds are driving off their high school parking lots with brand new Mercedes-Benzes, or BMWs. A couple of generations ago it was inconceivable for a seventeen year old to have a brand-new luxury vehicle. Some of my friends are extremely industrious, hardworking, and educated, and even they cannot afford vehicles like these. Amazing. It is not uncommon to hear of children as young as eight or ten years of age wanting their very own cell phones. I cannot even wrap my heard around this phenomenon.

When I was eight or ten years of age, the only time I used the phone was to say hello to my grandparents or aunts and uncles whenever they were on the phone. But it never even registered in my consciousness that I could want my very own phone. That concept just didn't exist. We had a family phone, and that was it. We had a couple of standard land line phones, in case we were in different parts of the house, but that was the extent of the telephone phenomenon. The most that my generation was criticized for using were the portable cassette players or radios with headphones, then known by the popular term Walkman.

I remember the then mayor of New York City, Ed Koch, was being interviewed on television. Among the many things he said, he began criticizing the "young people" (that included my generation) that would "walk around with these Walkmans, causing themselves to go deaf!" That was almost thirty years ago. In retrospect, having a cassette player strapped to my waist and enjoying music with headphones seems like nothing compared with the myriad of gadgetry that young people of today "must" have in order to fit in with the in-crowd at school. By the time I was enjoying music on cassettes, tapes had already been around a dozen years. Yet, the youth of today are being sold technological marvels that are obsolete within a year! I cannot keep up with these advances. The pressure to keep up with these advances in technology is incredible. And this planned obsolescence is part of the reason why young people are spending so much more money than my generation did when I was a child.

There has to be an upward limit, at which point a person says "enough." People have to ask themselves when is enough "enough." At what instant does a person realize that they've acquired enough? At one point does a person feel that they have "enough" of a home? At one point does a person feel that they have "enough" possessions in his or her home? And, at that point, one has to have, or develop, the ego strength to resist those social pressures to continue to spend money. I remember one young man in graduate school was wearing a nice shirt one day. I complimented him on it, and asked him where he had purchased the shirt. He told me that it had belonged to his father, and that the shirt was about 30 years old. At first glance, that shirt looked quite new and very stylish. There was nothing about that shirt that dated it to the early 1970s. It looked contemporary, clean and well-preserved. Yet, what impressed me about this young man was that he evidently was wise enough not to feel that just because a shirt is 30 years old doesn't mean that one can't wear it and enjoy it. Furthermore, and perhaps most importantly, both he and his father had taken good care of that shirt, and had kept it to near new condition.

Our society doesn't tolerate this practice very well. In our society, if something is several years old, out it goes. Out with the old, and in with the new, as they say. Our society has abandoned the practice of taking good care of older items and continuing to use those items years, if not decades, later. Imagine what would happen if more people practiced this. Clothing stores would begin to lose money, as would other areas of the economy. Our entire economic system cannot withstand the abandonment of the 'out with the old' practice.

The entire capitalist system that is embedded within our society demands that we throw away that which is 'obsolete' (by other people's standards) and to enthusiastically embrace that which is 'new'. I saw a news segment recently which talked about the fact that people in England are returning to the usage of compact cassettes. These are the same cassettes that have been around since the very early 1970s. The English find them cheaper, more reliable, and find no need to have the latest in sound system equipment. I still use cassettes. But corporate America continues to encourage millions of people to buy that which is newer and better. Someone recently told me that the iPod can hold thousands of songs in its memory. I don't even know thousands of songs! Perhaps not even hundreds! And, what happened to the entertainment of listening to the radio?

The extent to which our society pressures us to purchase that is which is new is amazing. I was on a website recently which was heralding the arrival of the *Back to the Future* movies on Blu-ray. The author of the on-line advertisement was eager to describe the clarity and resolution of the Blu-ray movies as opposed to their older 'regular' DVDs. The web page featured screen shots of the 'older' DVD movie, and, below it, the Blu-ray screen shots. Frankly, they looked pretty similar to me. Perhaps I was able to see more wrinkles on Christopher Lloyd's face. Is that why I should purchase one of these machines? So that I can see the wrinkles and blemishes on an actor's face more clearly? Corporate America seems to think so.

What troubles me is that no one wants to stand up and yell that the emperor has no clothes. That is to say, why isn't anyone (besides me) standing up and declaring how ludicrous this all really is? Are people afraid that they might seem 'unpatriotic'? If that's the case, is there anything truly unpatriotic about finding something that could be improved upon in society? I don't think so. Does a mother or father love his child any less when he or she offers constructive criticism? I see nothing subversive or unpatriotic in describing something which needs changing in society.

The most patriotic citizens have been the ones who dared to speak up and declare that something was not right, and needed to be corrected in our country. Therefore, I am speaking up in declaring that the corporate culture in this country is brainwashing millions of people to buy things they don't need. They have brainwashed millions of people into believing that they 'need' the newest gadget or car that is introduced. They have succeeded in making us think that our lives will be improved by the purchase of appliances that, in the end, do not save us as much labor as we were led to believe.

Are people any happier as a result of these purchases? Probably not. But they were duped into thinking so. Has the quality of our lives improved because of the introduction of the iPod or iPhone? Probably not. What the corporate mentality has done is truly nefarious. They have deluded us into believing that life will improve, somehow, almost magically, if we purchase their products. African American inner-city youth have even murdered each other just to have the latest set of sneakers! Words are not enough to allow me to express how I feel about that. Suffice it to say, that the capitalist system has succeeded the most vulnerable, and impressionable, in our society, to become, and behave, like animals.

I recently watched a video of people rushing into department stores on Black Friday, the day after Thanksgiving, of all days. The people rushing into the stores had a cattle like mentality, blindly running into the stores, and fighting with each other over the latest video game or appliance. One video even showed people fighting and clamoring to get the latest waffle maker. I am not joking. A waffle maker. What in the world is so important about a waffle maker that people will begin to shove each other in order to buy one?

I really don't understand this phenomenon. There were reports of injuries, and even one death, as a result of the stampede of people into the stores at midnight, or three o'clock in the morning. Mothers could clearly be seen with their toddlers in their arms, running through the crowds! It didn't seem to matter to these mothers that they were endangering their infants by putting them in a place where they could get easily trampled to death, but that they were also keeping their infants awake far past their bedtime.

I couldn't believe how the masses are brought down to the level of the animals in their behavior. Why would they rush into a store at three o'clock in the morning in order to buy a waffle maker? Why is so important that they have one? Watching the video, you would think that war had broken out, and that these people were scrambling to get water or medicine. Something truly life-saving. Even then, in an emergency, the best thing to do is to stay away from a mob. They can easily trample someone to death. That is precisely what happened in the death that I referred to above.

A security guard was trampled to death by the mob that stepped on him as they went berserk when the door at a store opened on Black Friday. Black indeed. For me, the name Black Friday is quite fitting. It is black because it shows the degree to which the masses have become brainwashed by corporate America. They are managing to get people to stay awake until the early hours of the morning and then, when the store doors open, getting them to rush into a store like mice, blindly grabbing item after item. It reminds me of a fumble in a football game; the mad scramble, and absolute chaos. At least football players are paid to scramble.

Yet, on Black Friday, people are paying for the experience! And they are paying for the experience with money they don't have! By one anti-spending advocate's calculations, people are still paying off their Christmas debt in May, five months later. I feel sorry for the people that have been duped like this. Their lives must be terribly empty. They then fill that emptiness with the (equally) empty promises that are made by corporate America. The promise is that these consumers will magically be happier by purchasing item after item.

The only people who are actually *happier* are those that are making money from the stampede of brainwashed individuals who trample over everyone else to buy a waffle maker at three in the morning. Yes, those fat cats at the top of the corporate ladder must be smiling indeed. They most likely have a smile from ear to ear, like a Cheshire cat. They succeeded. They managed to convince gullible herds of people that they absolutely need to go out and buy what they, corporate America, tells them to buy.

Most historians have marveled at how Adolf Hitler managed to convince millions of Germans that they needed to vote for him. He used the right language, the right words, and he appealed to people's emotions. Sure enough, he became the Chancellor of the German nation. But then, he managed to convince the Germans that they could, and should, take over Western Europe, and exterminate all Jews in the process. It seems inconceivable that a single person could convince the people who gave us Mozart, Beethoven, Goethe, and Werner van Braun, that they should embark on such a disastrous mission. And it was truly disastrous for the Germans. And yet, as we struggle to understand the Third Reich, our corporate leaders are brainwashing us in a similar manner. Thankfully, they are not convincing us to that we need to exterminate a certain race, or that we need to take over the Western Hemisphere. Yet, the type of brainwashing that Hitler used is, on some level, being used by the moguls of our capitalist system to convince millions of people to spend money they don't have.

I was recently driving home on one of the many freeways in Southern California. It was a Friday evening. I saw an impregnable line of cars heading over to another freeway. This line of cars was headed for the Inland Empire, due east by quite a few miles from Los Angeles. There are vast tracts of homes there. Mushroom communities. There are countless individuals who work in Los Angeles, and live in homes in the Inland Empire. However, what struck me was the sheer volume of people who are willing to commute from Los Angeles to the Inland Empire, merely to live in the two-story homes that are in abundance in the Inland Empire. The traffic was moving at about two miles per hour, and it was bumper to bumper.

At one point you could see an endless trail of red lights heading into the Inland Empire. It was a seemingly endless row of cars, being driven by individuals who bought into the idea that they needed a certain kind of home. They feel that they need their home to be of a certain size and square footage. They are willing to drive a very long commute, nothing short of two hours, to have this home. Is it worth it? My father, who was riding in the car with me, saw the seemingly infinite row of tail lights on the freeway headed east, toward the

Inland Empire. He commented that this is the reason why modern marriages are strained, or end in divorce. He commented that this is the reason that families are so fragmented and dysfunctional. Indeed.

Why do people do this to themselves? Why do people willingly stress themselves out, merely to have a 'nice' home? Is it human avarice? Is it the work of the human ego? Is it a need to fill emptiness inside? This is craziness in its absolute purest form. People are willing, happily, to submit to this daily commute? Obviously, these commuters feel that it is worth it. The fact that these commuters feel that it is 'worth it' to drive two hours in the morning, and two hours in the evening, merely to have a certain kind of home, is a testament to how effectively, and how completely, corporate America has brainwashed these individuals. They don't question it. Just like no one questioned Adolf Hitler's edicts. Are we any more enlightened than the millions who joined the Nazi Party?

In the end, I respect people's right to make their own choices. It is their right to commute five hours a day, if they want. It's their decision. That is part of living in a 'free' society. But, quietly, I marvel at how people have been duped and sold a bill of goods, and they are willing to live very stressful lives in order to get those goods. And all because someone, somewhere, and somehow, managed to convince them that it's worth it. What clever advertising. What amazing salesmanship on a mass level.

People are actually willing to cut back on the hours that they spend with their children, or their spouses, merely for the sake of having a house. They are willing to breathe the cancer-causing carbon monoxide on the freeways in order to live in one of these homes. And, they are willing to endure the stress of driving on the congested freeways of Southern California in order to own one of these houses. And, for anyone who has never driven on a California freeway before, the drivers tend to be quite aggressive. Therefore, it is not a leisurely drive along a scenic highway, with nothing to do but listen to nice music on the car radio.

Driving in Southern California can be a very unnerving activity. Cars zip in and out of the lanes on the freeways, and most people drive in a hurry, disregarding the speed limit. Tailgaters are an everyday occurrence. All the accidents that I observed have been caused because one driver was tailgating behind another driver. Thus, the commuters who drive from their homes in the Inland Empire to Los Angeles and back again are not enjoying a relaxing commute. You must be on guard at all times on the freeways in Southern California. If you look down or away for one second, you may very well find yourself smashing into the car in front of you. Corporate America has reduced us to behaving like rats in a maze, looking for the cheese in the shape of a big house and a fancy car.

It can be difficult indeed to understand the values that shape our society. Furthermore, it is not just the values in the United States that I question, but the values in other parts of the world as well. It is as if the values of our world are upside down. Recently, I learned that Lindsey Lohan was offered a substantial amount of money to host a television show in Germany. There is no clear reason why the young people in Germany should be idolizing someone who has clearly demonstrated a self-destructive lifestyle. Not only has she been self-destructive by abusing drugs, but she clearly shows no respect to the rules which govern probationary behavior, such as her assignment to volunteer at the Los Angeles County Morgue, which she repeatedly avoided. She also avoided therapy, claiming she could not afford it. Her behavior was clearly antisocial, and she was bent on resisting the rules by avoiding them. Yet, the young people in Germany are idolizing her.

This attention, and the offer of money, only serves to keep her behavior in place. The attention and money serve as positive reinforcement. Why should she be a polite and dutiful citizen when notoriety is clearly being rewarded? Why are people like her idolized in society? What redeeming qualities does someone like her demonstrate to make up for their notoriety? Is goodness boring? Is politeness out of fashion? Why is notoriety rewarded? Why is the appearance of someone like her being celebrated by young people? What is there to celebrate? Another example comes to light. As I was standing in line in a grocery store recently, I saw special editions of magazines eulogizing the late Whitney Houston.

Although her sudden death was truly unfortunate, our society is not asking the right questions. Instead of special and glossy magazines paying their tributes, our society should be asking some very real and pertinent questions, such as: Why are the women in the entertainment industry engaging in self-destructive behavior? One need only think of Paris Hilton, Britney Spears, Lady Gaga, Lindsey Lohan, Demi Moore, and, of course, Whitney Houston. Instead of asking why these women are losing their coping skills, our society idolizes them and memorializes them when they pass on. This is not exactly a new phenomenon. There have been others in the entertainment industry whose self-destructive lifestyle was well-known, and whose early deaths made them even more famous, such as James Dean, Marilyn Monroe, Jimmy Hendrix, Elvis Presley, and River Phoenix.

We need to find out what's wrong with the entertainment industry that breeds this kind of behavior. And yet, even if there is something about that industry that breeds this behavior, we cannot disregard the issue of personal choice. No one put a gun to these people's heads and forced them to use drugs. They willingly made their choices. But our society has to stop this undue adulation of these individuals. We need to stop making heroes and heroines out of them. They clearly need psychological help, and massive amounts of therapy. What we need to do is change our social values and the ideals that stem from those values. By doing so, we will cease to make heroes and heroines out of celebrities and rock stars who engage in self-destructive behavior. And, yet, while I have always felt uncomfortable giving too much credence to conspiracy theories,

I do feel that there is a subversive capitalist machination to what is happening. The entertainment industry is very large in the United States. It is one of largest of the world. The movie studios and the music industry are powerful entities. There are millions, if not billions, of dollars circulating in and out of both of these industries. They cannot afford to have their main cash-cow movies stars and singers appear bad or placed in an unfavorable light. That would upset the potential revenue that these industries are banking on with these entertainers. They have to market these entertainers as saintly.

Or, if it is discovered that someone famous has entered rehab, or is found to be using drugs, the entertainment industry will perhaps only portray that entertainer as a 'victim' of a bad childhood, but not as a grown adults who are making bad choices for themselves. Therefore, the executives in the movie studios and in the music industry cannot afford to lose public support of their main entertainers. If people were to lose interest in these entertainers, they would probably no longer watch their movies or listen to their music. This would thwart these executives' ability to make money off of a paying public. This is one of the many money-making schemes that underlie our society.

Capitalist America does not want you to see Demi Moore any differently than before – there is too much money behind her name. If anything, they want you to idolize her for her brave struggles against her 'difficulties', and to see her in an even better light than before. Therefore, whenever she films her next movie, they want even more people to go see it. They will then double her promotional tours across the talk show circuits, plugging her latest movie. People will then tune in to her appearances on the talk show circuit with voyeuristic zeal, wanting to know all of the gruesome details of drug rehab. Her problems are somehow more interesting as a result of her fame. If we learn that someone down the street is using drugs, most of us are unsympathetic and express an obvious distaste for that kind of lifestyle. Yet, whenever someone like River Phoenix is known to be using drugs, we watch and listen with a kind of thrill-seeking fascination. It is somehow less distasteful if a movie star is using drugs, as opposed to the man down the street.

We are moved to feel a certain amount of sympathy. That poor man! It's all of the pressures of Hollywood that caused him to turn to drugs. It's not his fault! He's a victim! We need to rally support for this individual. We need to feel sorry for him. And, of course, we need to continue to support his work and watch all of his future movies. His name is not tainted in the least. His reputation is not tarnished in the least. Look at Lindsey Lohan! It seems that all of the trouble she has caused only served to advance her career! But it is the massive and powerful movie and entertainment industry that wants us to think along these lines. At this point, it may seem like I have rambled far afield of my original theme, which revolved around the question of whether we need to be spending so much money, merely because our society wants us to do this.

Well, with regards to the movie and entertainment industry, our society does not want us to think anything negative about movie stars and entertainers in general, and they (their agents) will do whatever it takes to preserve their clients' reputations so that the gullible and impressionable public will continue to idolize and worship these movie stars and singers. This guarantees the bottom line: people will spend money where they are encouraged to spend money. Concert tickets will sell out for the ex-drug addict who sings at the Staples Center in Los Angeles. Movie ticket sales will skyrocket for the young movie star whose notoriety was more effective than anything a marketing guru could have devised.

We see this with sports stars as well. There have been numerous examples of famous athletes who are discovered to be using illegal steroids, and other performance-enhancing drugs. Later, their endorsements are used to make money and to market products with their notorious signature on the label. The very notion of a celebrity endorsement is also quite a phenomenon in our capitalist society. I recently watched some videos of people who flocked, literally running into a department store to purchase their Air Jordan sneakers. People were paying well over a hundred dollars for a pair, merely because they think that because it has Mr. Jordan's signature, that it must be a superior product.

One man hid in a trash can outside a mall entrance. When one of the persons who had purchased the new Air Jordans approached the mall entrance this man leaped out of the trash can and approached him with an offer to buy his Air Jordans. He offered him a whopping four hundred dollars for the shoes! Clearly, from the way this man was dressed, plus the fact that he was hiding in a trash can, it appears that he was from a lower socioeconomic level. And, yet, he was willing to pay four hundred dollars to pay for these shoes. I don't even want to wander in the direction of wondering how he was able to get the four hundred dollars to spend on shoes. Yet, that goes to show the power of celebrity endorsements. Would he have paid four hundred dollars if the shoes had nothing to do with Michael Jordan? Have we raised Mr. Jordan to demigod status by deifying anything he puts his signature on and are later willing to lay down hundreds of dollars to purchase a product that he supposedly uses?

Yet, the signatures of Sir Alexander Fleming, or Jonas Salk, go unnoticed. They do not seem to merit the adulation that an athlete has garnered. I wonder if any young people recognize the name of the late Neil Armstrong. Would his signature mean anything to a 14 year old? I seriously doubt it. That is the nature of our society. The heroes of yesterday are replaced rather quickly by the current offering of modern 'role models', so called. Of course, these people, whether they be rap singers, athletes, or drug-abusing movie stars, are the people that we are supposed to idolize, whether they deserve that adulation or not. They are raised to demigod status, whether they have done anything to deserve it or not.

Yet, the only reason that they are put on such a high pedestal is so that we, fools that we are, will buy their products, watch their movies, or go to their concerts. There is money to be made from their names. The masses have to be manipulated to worship these individuals. There is too much financial investment at stake. Too many people in high levels of capitalist America will lose money if we don't worship Lady Gaga or Queen Latifah. Capitalist America is banking on, and is investing in, our impressionable minds to believe that there is something magical or special about these entertainers, such that we will either pay hundreds of dollars for their endorsed products, or that we will continue to flood the arenas where they perform.

For decades, the "American Dream" consisted of a nice, trim home with a white picket fence, a dog, a station wagon, and 2.5 children. After the Second World War, countless commercials on television showed the lifestyle of the new American Family living out their Stepford existence, complete with ownership of a home in the suburbs, and the rest of the accoutrements of the American Dream. Television became the new and extremely powerful medium through which Americans were witnessing that which they felt they needed to emulate. The images were clear and alluring. The actors and actresses were well coiffed and were shown pulling into the driveway of their new home, one of countless homes being laid out in neat tracks in the late 1940s and early 1950s.

And, to make the images even more appealing was the fact that the people in the commercials looked *happy*. That was one of the cleverest forms of advertising that has ever been produced. Like Pavlov's dogs, countless television viewers became conditioned to equate happiness to the acquisition of the American Dream. People saw the actor playing the role of the father, and the actress playing the role of the mother, and they saw the big smiles on their faces. It caused the television viewers to believe that that happiness could be theirs, if only they could afford a home such as the one in the commercial. But it was not just the homes in these television commercials that had this appeal. It was the new appliances, such as the types of ovens and dishwashers that every housewife felt she absolutely needed to have.

These appliances were being touted as being "labor-saving devices" and so the appeal was being made to housewives in particular, who felt that if they could only purchase these new marvels of modern technology, then they could free themselves up for more meaningful work, or leisure. Of course, the women in these commercials also looked quite happy as they pushed a vacuum cleaner across the carpet, wearing nothing less than high heels, a full dress, and a big grin. In a sense, what was being promoted was an *entire lifestyle* based on the acquisition of material items. The new tract home in the suburbs. The new station wagon or family car. The oven, dishwasher, and vacuum cleaner. Televisions. And automatic dinners thanks to frozen T.V. Dinners. No more having to cook dinner after a long day!

It was a complete form of living that was pre-packaged and gift-wrapped by corporate America. All of this promised the happiness that it was supposed to produce by virtue of the happiness that the actors and actresses evinced in the commercials. And it worked! Scores of veterans and their families moved to the suburbs, quiet enclaves where one could live without the racket of city life. The suburbs themselves became another "thing" that people sought. Why would anyone want to live in a noisy, grimy city when one can live in the outskirts where no one will disturb you? As these tract homes began to be sold, so was the idea of living out the dream life being shown on television. Appliances and televisions soon became staples in every American home. However, one of the most insidious aspects of this entire marketing scheme is that within the plan to sell people the idea that an entire lifestyle could be purchased, it also began to include the phenomenon of *planned obsolescence*. Corporate American figured out that if they could sell a product, then surely they could go back to the drawing board and make the product better, or faster, or sexier.

Therefore, when newer makes of automobiles were introduced, people began to feel the pressure to keep up with everyone else and obtain these newer vehicles. Similarly, when color television was introduced, it caused a similar reaction. Why would you want to watch television shows on black and white television when you could watch them in color? Therefore, the earlier generations of cars, homes, and appliances first being marketed in the television commercials of the 1950s were now being replaced by faster cars, bigger homes, and better, more advanced appliances. People could purchase vinyl records of their favorite music. However, vinyl records were replaced by 8-Track tapes. And, 8-Track tapes suffered a short time span as they were later replaced by compact cassette tapes, which had already been in existence for some time.

This pattern continued unabated in corporate and consumer circles. Why use a conventional oven when you can just pop your meal into a microwave oven and, *voilà*! It's ready in minutes, instead of hours. Don't worry if you can't watch your favorite television shows when they come on late at night, as you can now record them on a Video Cassette Recorder, or VCR! They're programmable, so all you have to do is program it to record your show, and you can drift off to sleep and let the VCR do all the work! The very notion that you could now watch movies in your home was revolutionary! People were using video disks, then the ubiquitous VCR, and finally the DVD. However, even DVDs are now in the endangered technology species list as they are being overtaken by Blu-ray players.

This type of marketing, in which new, better, smaller, more efficient technology is being sold to the masses has kept scores of people virtual slaves to the newer forms of technology which are now coming out practically every year. I am not certain if this plays upon people's fears not to be left alone, or if this is a carryover from our childhoods, when we always wanted to be part of the in-crowd. And this will be explored later in this book. Suffice to say that whatever trigger or nerve needs to be pushed or struck in order to get people to act, corporate American has found that nerve and has mastered the way that it can activate that nerve and cause people to go running into stores to purchase the latest gadget or appliance. It may seem like a literary device or exaggeration to describe people running into stores.

Yet, it is a well-known fact that on Black Friday, the day after Thanksgiving; people go running into stores at full gallop. The fact that it takes place after Thanksgiving, of all days, is also quite striking, and will be elaborated on further in the book. It is nothing short of hypocrisy that people hold Thanksgiving dinners, and give thanks for what they have, and then rush out the next morning for more things to buy. People have been seriously injured when the mobs run into the stores and they begin to trample over each other. It is almost shameful that we, as humans, would act this way. It brings us down to the level of the animals.

When I was a child, and it was time for me to feed my dog and I would for whatever reason feed him indoors, if the sliding door was open just one inch, he could smell the food and would begin to push open the sliding door, which was very heavy, and would get into a feeding frenzy, knowing that his tummy was soon going to be full of pooch chow. He would manage to fully open the sliding door and push his way in, and head straight for his food bowl. It was always fun for me to observe this phenomenon. Of course, I dismissed it because of the fact that he was a dog, an animal. However, when I hear the reports of people causing stampedes when stores open before dawn on Black Friday, it causes me to feel that we, as humans are behaving no different than the animals. Why do people feel that they have to be at the stores at that time of the morning?

Furthermore, with the ease and availability of on-line shopping, why would anyone go out into freezing weather, only to rush into a store to buy merchandise that cannot be afforded anyhow, except through credit? Yet, this is the type of slavery I will be demonstrating throughout this book. The people who run into those stores have become true slaves to a very clever system of marketing that has all but managed to make us believe that we cannot be truly *happy* unless we run out to buy the latest items that are being sold in stores. The pastor at my church has described this marketing phenomenon as being a state of mind "where happiness is only a purchase away." But, the frightening part is that so many people have become brainwashed and believe this. And, if you watch these television commercials closely, they have not changed all that much since the 1950s.

The people portrayed still smile and look quite happy in these sound bites. The new 2012 automobile is still rolling into a driveway of a home that is not that distinct from the tract homes of 60 years ago. What is different, however, is that the home is indeed larger, even though the family in the commercial may have only two children. The automobile is more computerized from the cars of the 1950s. Therefore, even though the size of the average American Dream family may still be roughly the same size, the message is clear: you need more to be happy than the families being portrayed on television in the 1950s. It is not enough that children sit in the backseat of long car drives and find ways to distract themselves, or nap, but now they can watch television while Dad or Mom drives the family minivan.

Of course, while they watch television in the back seat of the family minivan, they are being shown television commercials showing the latest car, or computer, or iPhone, and they become the next set of consumers who have become primed by corporate America, and they grow up believing, truly believing, that they must have these goodies in order to be happy. It is now well-known that corporate America catches us at birth and doesn't let us go until we die. From womb to tomb, we are in the hands of clever marketers who almost decide for us what we will be buying, and how much, and how often, and for what reason. It takes a lot of courage to decide not to play this game. And, what is truly disturbing and worrisome is that it is not a game. People have committed suicide when they reached a level of shameful and insurmountable debt that they knew they could not pay off, and felt too embarrassed to declare bankruptcy.

It may seem that in our time of war, crime, disease, and poverty (all of which are not new problems, by the way) that a discussion of debt, or the dangers of credit, may seem off-scale, in a sense. A book about people's slavery to materialism may seem trivial by comparison. When American soldiers are coming home from the Middle East in coffins and the Department of Homeland Security is scanning the horizon for signs of another attack, it may seem insignificant to have a discussion about materialism. Yet, it is a necessary discussion. And there is a connection between the two. Perhaps if more people were to stop paying attention to what's on sale at JCPenny, and begin to pay more attention to the war, and its human cost, perhaps people might actually begin lobbying for a quick end to the international conflicts in which we find ourselves.

Even if people feel that we must go and fight in another country, this type of national discourse can happen only if people let go of their slavery to materialism and focus their energies on more important things. Other issues, such as the environment, also warrant serious consideration, particularly given the fact that our rampant materialism has been one of the reasons for the degradation of our natural resources. The cutting down of the rainforests in South America, and the smog, and pollution in our rivers and oceans, all have their roots, on some level, to humanity's insistence to certain material goods, and material comforts. What mankind has to deal with are the long- and short-term consequences of corporate greed, on the one hand, and our large-scale materialistic desires, on the other.

It not just the environment that suffers, but people as well. I recently watched a documentary about sweat shops in Third World countries that produce clothing for major clothing distributors, such as Gap, and others. It was appalling to see how people are being treated, all in the name of having brand-name clothing. When people begin to place more importance on the label of their clothes, rather than care about the conditions of the workers who manufacture their clothes, then something is grossly wrong with our society. This speaks volumes about where we are in our greed as consumers, and the greed being displayed by corporate America.

However, I truly believe that there is hope for this seemingly hopeless situation. The recession in which we find ourselves is fertile ground, paradigmatically speaking, for us as Americans to begin the process of carving out for ourselves new values and a new sense of what truly matters in life. This book will serve as a guide and as a source of inspiration for a new way of living. Life is about so much more than the toys we buy or the cars we drive. Life is about relationships. Human relationships. It's about connecting to other people on a deep and spiritual level. And, it's about service to others, our fellow man, and to the Earth. This is a time when we must do whatever we must in order to preserve the dwindling natural resources we have left at our disposal. If we don't begin to think beyond our own wish for material possessions, the resources of the Earth will truly become endangered, and future generations will pay the price. Let this be the dawn of a new era for us as citizens, when we can let go of our need to acquire things and instead begin to look beyond ourselves at what is best for our collective humanity.

The next portion of the book is comprised of singular activities whose value and essence can be incorporated into a frugal lifestyle. The following activities were chosen because I feel that they represent a free, or low-cost, alternative to the high price of entertainment to which most people have become accustomed. The list is not intended to be exhaustive, and of course, it may be modified to be better suited to fit the needs of individual tastes and preferences. Not everyone will enjoy all of the activities that I have listed here, but, for the most part, many of these are fun and creative ways to live life without having to spend a lot of money. I have enjoyed a great many of these activities and continue to do so on a regular basis. They are intended to bring the reader back to a simpler form of living, one based on nature, family, community, the great outdoors, and a spiritual gracefulness. They have been placed into broad categories, thus providing a broad spectrum of activities that can be enjoyed in different parts of our lives.

PART II
Enjoyable Low-Cost or Free Activities

Category I

Spiritual Activities

LEARN TO MEDITATE

Meditation can be a wonderful way of relieving stress. The art of meditation entails letting go of the cares and worries of the day, and allowing the mind to empty itself. There are many ways to meditate. The classic form involves sitting quietly for some time. It can be a few minutes, or it can be a much longer period of time. For those of you who are new to this form of relaxation, here are some suggestions for meditating: Find a quiet place where you will be undisturbed. Wear loose, comfortable clothing. If possible, wear cotton clothes. Cotton breathes a little better than artificial fabrics, and will thereby keep your body cool. And, make sure that your clothes are not tight or constricting. I normally wear shorts when I am at home, so you may want to wear either shorts or loose pants.

Sit with your legs crossed, one on top of the other. Make sure that your back is straight. Pay attention to your breathing. Take deep slow breaths. Allow your hands to rest comfortably on your legs or knees. Close your eyes. Try to empty your mind of all thoughts and distractions. Let go of all thoughts of work and the bills. Let go of all concerns about your finances, or your family. Try to go inward, deep within yourself. Go toward that center where your soul resides. Tap into the stillness that is created in that center. Keep focusing on your breathing. Make sure that you are breathing deeply. Many people breathe in a shallow manner when they are anxious. This restricts the flow of oxygen to the brain. Continue to empty your mind.

Some people meditate more effectively when they focus on a particular word, or mantra. A mantra is a word or phrase that allows you to meditate more deeply. The purpose or goal is to focus on the word or phrase being repeated. It can be any word you choose. Some people like to meditate to the word "Love" and other people choose the word "God," and so on. Choose a word that feels right for you. Or, you might choose not to use any words at all. You may choose to simply "be." In our society, people are so used to being busy that they forget how to just "be." Allow yourself to just be with nature, or to be with God. Try to set aside time each day for meditating. Over time, it will become more and more natural to you. Be patient, and allow this practice to develop.

LIVE A LIFE OF ZEN

One of the techniques utilized by Zen monks in Asia is that of practicing the art of Zen. This practice revolves around being mindful of whatever you are doing, and being at one with the activity. In our overachieving society, we are constantly being asked to multitask. This involves balancing multiple projects or ideas, all at once. We are asked to accomplish several things at the same time. One can readily see this in the corporate world. People may be at their computer, looking at data, while on the phone with a customer, and jotting down data on a notepad, while glancing at the text messages piling up on their iPhone.

The amount of productivity that is expected of modern employees is, at times, unreasonable. The more that is piled upon the mind, the less effective the mind will be at performing any one task. Yet, that is the crazy nature of the modern working environment in which so many employees find themselves, all the while feeling that they have no choice but to submit to these demands. However, Zen allows us a way to counter these demands by allowing us to focus on one thing at a time. It may be a good idea to differentiate between the ability to do this at home, and the inability to do this at your work, where you may indeed be faced with multiple projects to complete. Therefore, consider this an adjunct to your meditation practices.

Begin this habit by focusing completely one what you are doing at any one point in time. Too many of us continue the multitasking even when we come home from work. We become so accustomed to the multitasking that we do at work that we bring that habit home with us on our time off. We allow ourselves to continue in that habit, even when we don't need to at the end of the day. Granted, many parents come home to hungry children who need to do their homework, and a pet that needs to be fed and groomed, and a dirty kitchen and bathroom that need to be cleaned.

I recognize that there are numerous demands placed upon the working classes, and wives and mothers usually end up taking the brunt of these chores and responsibilities. This is why the art of developing a Zen state of mind takes time. Train your mind to focus only on the shirt you are ironing, or the dishes you are washing. Focus solely on the work of vacuuming the carpet. With time, you will be able to focus your mind solely on the task at hand, rather than the crazy-making involved in multitasking.

Light up Incense

Incense can be a wonderful way to create a monastic environment in your home. Thankfully, there are many types of incense which can be purchased, and many of these varieties can be purchased at very reasonable prices. Some fragrances are simply wonderful, others less so. Thus, you should find a fragrance that works best for you. There are several types of incense. There are little cones that you can burn. Simply light the tip of the cone with a match, and then blow it out. The smoke from the burning end of the cone will fill the air with a calming fragrance. There are also the stick varieties, which likewise need only the tips to be lighted, and the smoke does the rest. The third category of incense is comprised of little nuggets of dried resin that provide a wonderful fragrance by placing the tiny nuggets of incense on top of burning charcoals. This is the type of incense normally seen in churches.

Burning any one of these types of incense can be a wonderful way of re-creating a monastic feel in your home or garden. Incense is a way of connecting us to the more ethereal states of mind upon which our spirituality rests. Burning incense can also be a wonderful adjunct to your meditation exercises. I have meditated while burning incense and the effect is truly calming and spiritual. Incense takes us away from the material world and transports us to that higher plane of existence where matter drops away, and the spirit takes over. Of course, incense can have more practical applications as well. It can be a way of refreshing the air in your home.

In today's world of chemical and artificial air sprays and air fresheners, burning incense can be a wonderful "Old World" change of pace, rather than use the more commercially available air fresheners. Burning incense has a more natural scent, and has no chemical ingredients that are toxic to the lungs. Try one type or variety, and, if you find that you are not satisfied with the effect, perhaps you may want to try several others. Or, you may want to try scented oils, which are also burned over a little candle. Either way, scented oil, or incense can be a very sensual addition to your day, and they have a very calming effect on the mind as well. You may also want to try it at different times to create a different atmosphere, or effect. Incense at bedtime can be a very gentle way of training the mind to relax and get ready for a very soothing night's rest. Choose what feels right for you.

WRITE YOUR OWN PRAYER

Many of us hail from different religious backgrounds. And, in some of these religious roots, we were instructed in various forms of prayer. We were told what to say, how to say it, and at what time of the day or night to say it. Therefore, we were raised with a rather automatic, or robotic, form of prayer. It was institutionalized and regimented. There were rules surrounding it. And, while it may bring great comfort to many to find that the prayers they said as children are still being read aloud in unaltered form, this can also be somewhat stifling for others. Perhaps there needs to be a balance between reciting a prayer in rote form, and finding other, more creative ways of expressing your spiritual needs.

One manner of inculcating this creativity is the art of writing your own prayers. They need not even be full-fledged prayers. They can be petitions of sorts. You may simply want to write down the changes that you would like to see in your life, read the message aloud, and then toss the paper into the fireplace. I once purchased my partner an exquisite prayer bowl. It is made of metal, is only about six inches in diameter and only a few inches in height. However, the purpose of the bowl is to be the receptacle for hand-written prayers that are placed inside of the bowl. This can be part of your daily ritual. To save money, you may want to search in your kitchen for a bowl or jar that is not being

Write down any thoughts, meditations, mantras, or prayers you may have in your mind. Then, designate the bowl or jar you choose as the recipient of your prayers and heartfelt messages. This can be a way of letting go of your feelings and thoughts. Own them, and then write them down. You may then choose to meditate on them for a while. But, by placing them in the bowl or jar, you are then allowing yourself the ability to let go of these thoughts. Own them, and then release them. Take ownership of them, and then offer them up to the gods. You may have a spiritual belief system; however, give up your written prayers to the god of your choice. But the important thing is that you offer these prayers up as an offering, a supplication. You may want to burn incense as part of your ritual. Write down your heartfelt prayers and then offer them up to a higher power to whom you feel fealty and love. Make sure that your prayers are written, not typed. They must be from the heart.

ENJOY CANDLELIGHT

Candles can be wonderful way to increase your spiritual devotion each day. Lighting a candle can be part of your daily spiritual practices. A candle represents purity, and singleness of mind. It can also represent peace and tranquility. However, lighting a candle can be a way of offering a devotion to God. The practice of lighting a candle can be a way of creating a monastic environment in your home. Thankfully, there are many different types of candles. Some are short, wide candles, and others are of the tall, tapered variety. As with incense, try to find a type of candle that best suits your needs. If safety is a prime consideration, you may want to try small "tea light" candles. If you have small children in your home, you may want to wait until they are asleep before lighting your candles.

You may also want to try lighting candles in different parts of your home, such as your garden, or in your bathroom. A very soothing and sensuous practice is to turn off of the lights in your bathroom, and light small candles that you can place at the edges of your bathtub. Allow yourself to slip into a nice, warm bath. Soft, scented candles should be the only source of light illuminating your bath. Some people have small private altars in their home, or a place where they practice their daily spiritual devotion. You may want to consecrate a special area of your home. This will preferably be a place where you will face the least distractions. Also consider placing your incense burner in that place as well. This can be your spirituality nook.

A candle can be a wonderful accompaniment to a quiet moment of personal prayer. The soothing light from the candle can be a way to remind yourself to still your mind and to quiet your heart. The flame in a candle always points up. This can be your metaphor for always pointing your spirit and your heart up to God. Given the fact that many candles are scented, their fragrance can be a substitute for incense. Therefore, with a scented candle, you can experience both forms of spiritual supplementation at once. A candle flame is normally silent. Therefore, this can also serve as a metaphor for the importance of remaining still and silent as you contemplate the candle flame. Embrace the quietude. Embrace the silence. Turn off the noise of the day as you light a candle. Consider this part of your time alone, and it is to be devoted to you every bit as much as it is being devoted to God.

CREATE YOUR OWN RITUAL

The pastor at my church recently described how he has developed a daily ritual of getting up every morning for an hour of prayer and silence. In essence, this is his hour of meditation. He practices this daily and it helps to steady him for the work and challenges in the day ahead. It keeps him focused and grounded. Without it, he might very well feel stressed out over the myriad responsibilities that his work brings him. You may want to consider the art of having a daily spiritual ritual. Even the word "spiritual" has the word *ritual* inside of it. Set time aside each day when you will be undisturbed. You may want to light a candle and perhaps some incense. Allow your mind to be emptied of all thoughts and anxieties. Train your mind become still and steady.

Daily ritual has an important heritage in the monastic tradition. Monks and the clergy regularly incorporate daily ritual into their daily routines. You may want to play a piece of music that brings you relaxation or tranquility. I sometimes play music by Enya, whose soft, sweet, musical strains have a spiritual quality all their own. However, you may want to play the type of music that appeals to you. There may also be different times of the day that are better for you to incorporate a daily spiritual ritual. For some, the mornings are an ideal time to set up a ritual. For others, the evenings are better. You decide. A strong case could be made for either time. The mornings have a wonderful peacefulness all their own. However, who hasn't been transfixed by the beauty of a colorful sunset?

Some people even choose the middle of a work day and set it aside for their rituals. I had a supervisor who goes to a church across the street from her workplace and listens to the free music played at the church every Wednesday. This has become a ritual of sorts for her. Therefore, take time to decide what would create the ideal ritual for you. It can be simple, or it can be elaborate. You may want to meditate while on the train to work! Ultimately, you may want to experiment with different approaches to daily ritual and then find the one that suits you best. It may take some time to find the right ingredients, so be patient. It may take time to find the ritual which feels good for you. It may involve some switching around. Keep in mind that a ritual does not have to be fixed. You may want to have silence on some mornings and have music on others, or silence and prayer on other days. Let your spirit guide you.

READ A SACRED TEXT

Part of a ritual may involve reading a piece of sacred text. There are all types of sacred texts, spanning almost all of the major known religions of the world. You may come from a Buddhist tradition, or a Christian tradition, or a Judaic background. Sacred texts allow us to connect with the ideas, thoughts and conceptions of our faith backgrounds. Reading a sacred text connects us to the past, grounds us in the present, and prepares us for the future. In our secular world, we are bombarded with all types of mindless chatter and superficial conversation. We send and receive text messages. We send and receive e-mails. We call people on our cell phones just to see what they are doing. I have been in so many venues and have observed other people. Time and again I will hear a person on her or his cell phone, asking another person, "What are you doing?" Upon hearing the answer, the person then reciprocates and states in reply, "Me? Oh, I'm at the supermarket, looking at bananas."

In our modern, technology-driven society, we have become so used to mindless conversation and empty exchanges of pseudo-conversation that we have lost touch with what really matters in life. This is why reading a sacred text can be so valuable. It allows us to re-connect with words that give life its meaning. We are put in touch with concepts that go beyond the bananas on sale at the supermarket. Reading a sacred text puts us in touch with those who were our spiritual pioneers. You may want to read text that is part of an accepted, mainstream religion, or, you may want to read a text that is more abstract, even mysterious in origin. I recently ran across an ancient text known as the Kolbrin Bible, whose origins are mysterious.

There is much debate as to whom or how it was written. Nevertheless, you may want to explore the world's religions, both mainstream and fringe, and try to find a piece of sacred text that you find appealing. You don't even have to join the religion in order to enjoy their sacred writing. If you simply don't find any sacred texts that appeal to you, another option may be to write a piece of sacred text yourself. It may be a prayer, or a spiritual supplication. You may simply want to write down what you believe to be the order of the cosmos, or your own spiritual beliefs. Another idea may be for you to fashion your own spiritual manifesto, or an outline of all that you believe to be true about our universe and its Creator.

CREATE A HOME ALTAR

For those of you who may wish to practice your spirituality at home rather than in a church, one way of doing this is to create your very own altar. Some cultures have developed this practice more than others. Many Catholics have a private devotional altar at home. They place a statue of the Blessed Virgin Mary at the center, and place flowers or candles all around the periphery. For those of you who are not Catholic, you may want to consider an altar that can be situated in a nook in your home. It does not have to involve much space. You may want to find a candle, or a passage from a sacred text, or an incense burner, or have all of these together, and place them in a corner of a room where they will be undisturbed.

It does not even have to be an item of religious significance. It can be a photograph of a loved one, or a crystal, or even a flower. Use whatever inspires you to deepen your spiritual faith. Some people use little statues. You may want to use a rock. I once knew someone who kept a piece of petrified wood, and it was displayed rather prominently. Remember, when it comes to your own religious beliefs, or spiritual views, you don't always have to live by a set of rules. If a piece of wood connects you to God, then use it. If a small tea light candle connects you to God, then use that. You may want to switch it up. Try using a candle on one day, and a stone another day. The decision is yours.

But make sure that whatever form of altar you choose, it is one that inspires you to develop a deeper faith. You may want to change your home altar in sync with the changing seasons. You may want a flower to represent the new growth of spring. A photograph of a family vacation may signify the vacations that have been taken in the summertime. A leaf or a few brown, orange, and red leaves may represent fall, or autumn. A Nutcracker doll may represent winter. At any rate, use the iconography that inspires you to develop a deeper faith. Some churches in the Eastern Orthodox faith have beautiful golden iconography. You may want to print a color photo of these icons and use that as part of your home altar. Art museums also sell post cards with this imagery. Those postcards can also be part of your home altar. Be creative. Let your spirit guide your decision-making paradigm.

There is no right or wrong answer. Your heart will inform you when you have found the right images for your home altar. Visit a Different Church. Growing up as a Catholic, one of the distinct pleasures I have had is being able to visit other Catholic churches. Even when I visited England, which is a predominantly Protestant country, I had the good fortune to attend mass at Westminster Cathedral. It was a truly beautiful experience. As part of your spiritual growth and development, I recommend visiting other churches of your same faith. Some churches have a small, intimate, or "cozy" atmosphere, whereas others are large, cavernous and more imposing.

TRY A NEW RELIGION

For those of you who feel that you need an entirely new perspective on your faith, you may want to take the big leap and try a new religion. This may very well be a life-changing experience. A new religion may mean that you will see things differently. Former gods may be reduced to mere prophets. New gods may be worshiped. It all depends on how far afield you go. I went from being a Roman Catholic (which I suppose I always will be in my heart of hearts), to being an Episcopalian. However, although it meant going from Catholic to Protestant, the actual liturgy and service remained essentially the same. Even the wording remained the same. However, this still falls within the purview of Christianity.

What I am referring to here is an entirely new religion, on the order of going from Buddhist to Judaism, or the switch from Christianity to Shintoism. You may want to study the religion that you are considering switching to thoroughly before making the plunge. There may be aspects of a new religion you may not like. For instance, you may want to consider whether a new religion may impede your wish to marry someone from outside that religion. There are other rules you may want to keep in mind. There may be dietetic rules that you may have to adhere to in a new religion. For example, I love bacon and Canadian ham, so I could never be an Orthodox Jew. Or, you may have to believe in something entirely different from what you were brought up to believe. Therefore, do your homework.

You may want to start by reading about the religion you are considering. Go to the library, or order some books which describe the religion, right down to its smallest details. In the end, the choice is yours. I have met people who changed religions and seemed quite happy. I have heard of others who changed religions and were not happy with the result. Therefore, if you are going to change religions, read and study as much about it as you can, and visit one of their churches, or temples. Talk to people from that faith, both the laity and the clergy. Read their creeds. Find out what they believe, and that which they don't believe. And, remember, even after you have joined, you can always leave if it doesn't feel right. However, it may also turn out to be a transformative experience which enriches it far beyond than you may have imagined it could, or beyond the religion with which you were raised.

TALK TO A MINISTER, PRIEST, OR SPIRITUAL LEADER

In our society, we are constantly faced with the stressors of modern daily life. Most of us become stressed out and need someone with which we can share or unload our troubles and get a fresh perspective. Religious leaders can provide just that. They can be the counselor you may need them to be. Most of them are wonderful listeners and can offer you a fresh perspective you may not have thought of on your own. A religious leader may also offer you comfort in a way that, perhaps, a standard psychotherapist may not be able to impart. This is why you may want to give a priest or minister the benefit of the doubt and schedule a half hour to talk to him or her. Perhaps your marriage is shaky. Perhaps you are being affected by the economy. Or, perhaps you may be a caregiver to someone who has cancer. Whatever burden you are carrying, you may want to get hold of a leader in your church and talk to him or her. I have known religious leaders who were very good and impartial listeners. Others were not. Some were unbiased, and others have a distinct and obvious slant to their perspective.

Therefore, you may want to be very selective in whom you confide in when you choose someone. What you may also do is to have a spiritual leader be one among several people with whom you consult when you are stressing over the circumstances in your life. Remember that religious leaders have a responsibility to uphold the religion that they represent. Therefore, be mindful that the perspective that you hear may not always be 100% neutral. They may very well be attempting to toe the line in terms of their own religious beliefs. Nevertheless, someone who has become a spiritual leader has most likely gained enough education and worldly experience that they may be able to give you some very valuable advice. It is very unlikely that they will charge you money.

Therefore, in the current economic climate in which we find ourselves, it may be a wise choice to look for a pastor, priest or other holy person with whom you can have a dialog. By being respectful of their views, there is a good chance that they will be respectful to you as well. You may want to talk to that person more than once. However, a spiritual leader may also refer you to other community resources that may help you, such as the nearest drug rehabilitation center or other such forms of personal assistance or need.

CATEGORY II

Home and Hearth

REORGANIZE YOUR FURNITURE

One of the most enjoyable activities that I performed as an adolescent was to re-arrange my room. I would literally transform my room. My bed would be moved from one side of the room to the other. I would also move my desk to another location, perhaps close to the window. This was great fun, and it involved no outlay of money. After the activity was completed, it was truly rewarding to take a shower, and then lie down in my "new" room. I felt like I was in a different home. It was as though this was someone else's house. You may want to think about how your living room would look like if you were to move the furniture around. This is also a wonderful way to clean. You will be amazed at the amount of dust and filth that accumulates under a couch or under a table. This may involve several hours, so be sure to do this on a day when you are not working. You may also want to take out a measuring tape and make sure that the changes you want will fit in the space that you have.

Some spaces are rather confined, and so there may only be so many ways that the furniture can be moved. It may involve some trial and error. You may even discover a hidden talent for interior decorating that you never knew you had! Redecorating or reorganizing a room in your home may bring about a welcome change from the doldrums of having the same layout all the time. Perhaps you may want your bed closer to the window, so that you can bask indulgently when the first rays of the sun begin peeking through the window. Or you may elect to have your bed closer to your closet so that you can literally roll out of bed and get into the clothes that you select for the day. A thrift store, like your local Salvation Army, may be a great location to purchase low-cost paintings.

One of my friends has purchased beautiful works of art at thrift stores, and most of them were already framed! Or you may want to find new lamps or a dresser at a thrift store. By the end of the weekend, you may end up having what amounts to a brand-new look for your home or apartment. It's important to keep life fresh and free from stagnation. Life is too short to maintain an unexciting form of existence. Liven up your home by changing things up a bit! You may even want to experiment with a new type of décor, such as a Polynesian or Hawaiian look, or perhaps a more maritime look, such as what one may find in sleepy New England villages and cottages.

TURN OFF THE ELECTRONICS

We live in an age when there is constant noise and images coming at us from multiple directions. People are plugged into their iPads, iPhones, Netbooks, and other such technological marvels. As handy as these devices may seem, they have also taken over most of our free time. I was at the car wash not long ago. It was a beautiful, sunny day. I turned my car in to be washed, and I walked over to the plastic chairs that are lined up in a row against the far wall in the parking lot. I sat down and decided to absorb the warm rays of the sun that were shining down upon me that day. A young woman came over and sat down a couple of chairs away from me. I closed my eyes in order to take a sort of mini-nap. I opened my eyes briefly and threw a surreptitious sideways glance at her. She had pulled out her Blackberry or other such gadget and was busily punching the buttons on the keypad. It was an unusually beautiful day, and there was a soft breeze blowing.

Blessed with such beautiful weather, I could not get over why someone would want to be plugged in like this. I do realize that there are times when one must contact a supervisor, and there can be a few other such exigencies that demand immediate action. However, what is of concern to me is the fact that a car wash lasts only about ten or fifteen minutes. Why have we become so uncomfortable with the idea of letting go of our gadgetry even for that period of time? It is as if so many young people wouldn't have any idea what to do if they were not plugged into their portable computing machines.

It seems that people today, particularly young people, have lost touch with the ability to simply close their eyes and enjoy the feeling of the warmth of the sun, and feeling the cool breeze blow through their hair. These more 'sensual' enjoyments are entirely lost on the current generation of college students and people in their 30s. Try shutting off your iPod, or iPhone, or Blackberry and see how you feel. Are you going through withdrawal? Allow the anxiety to turn it on again to pass. This anxiety will diminish. You can go an entire day without your gadgetry. Our parents were able to go without a personal computer for years, and they somehow managed to survive. Try and see if you can increase the time without your gadgetry. Take your dog for a walk instead. Lie on the beach and enjoy the sun. Go to a movie. Spend time with a friend. There is life beyond text messaging.

DISINHERIT AND DECLUTTER

One way of getting a new lease on life is to streamline your home. If these challenging economic times are inspiring you to begin living a simpler life, then a wonderful way to begin is to start decluttering your home. Give yourself an entire day to begin looking at every room, one by one. Look in the closets. Are there clothes that you don't wear anymore, or never did to begin with? I have heard so many stories of people who have a closet full of clothing that still has the price tags attached! They were never worn! It happens to the best of us.

However, what is needed is a moment of reckoning. You need to ask yourself whether you will really ever need to continue keeping, dusting, and otherwise caring for clothes that you either don't want to wear, are out of style, or have simply fallen out of favor with you. Many of us have bought clothing on impulse. We saw some item of clothing, and thought it would look good on us. We got home, and, something happened. Perhaps it was the mood we were in when we were at the store. Yet, so many of us have tried on the clothes at home only to discover that we don't like the way they look. And, similarly, many of us have stowed them in the closet thinking that we might 'warm up' to these clothes 'one day'. That day rarely comes.

What is needed is a healthy dose of self-honesty. Next, look at your inventory of shoes. How many of us still have shoes in their original boxes under our beds, or stacked in the closet? Ask yourself: how many shoes do I really need? Rather than become part of a culture of excess, become part of a culture of giving. Take some of the shoes that you know, deep down, will never be worn again and take them to your local Goodwill or Salvation Army. However, don't stop with your excess or worn out clothing. Next go to your garage or tool shed. How many hammers or cans of paint do you need? Check your kitchen. Do you really need six sport bottles? Can you make do with only a couple? Look at the rest of your home? How many sets of china do you really need? This is the time when you can shake off the habit of years of excess spending and acquisition. I don't think that anyone is innocent of these habits. Even the most frugal persons I have seen also had a surplus of one kind or another. You can shed this excess domestic weight and start anew. Make this the start of a new era of decluttering. It is an extremely liberating feeling.

DON'T THROW IT AWAY—PATCH IT UP

It may seem like a direct contradiction to state that you should declutter your home, only to state in the next section that you should not throw things away. Let me illustrate the distinction. When I mentioned that you should throw things away that you don't need, I was referring to clothing that will never be worn, or shoes that will never be enjoyed, as well as other items that were purchased on impulse and were never utilized one way or another. These are the things that contribute to dead weight and only add clutter to your home.

What I am referring to here is the fact that, as a society, we have not only become a culture of over consumption, we have also become a culture of throwing perfectly good things away in order to get the latest, or most recent version of an appliance or electronic gadget. The marketplace is full of people wanting you to throw out your old Kindle in order to purchase the latest version. Last year's iPhone? Forget it! You need to purchase the latest model with all the new apps! Out with the old, and in with the new! That is the pervasive mentality in corporate America. The moguls who design these products want you to continue to keep spending your hard-earned money.

One of the ways that they can convince you to do this is to get you to believe, or should I say trick you into believing, that you need to throw out your old items so that you can make room for the newer versions. Stop and think about this. Do you really need the new Kindle Reader? Or can you make do with actual paper books instead? And, instead of purchasing books, could you not check them out of the library instead? Does your current vacuum cleaner do the job of cleaning your carpets? Do you really need the newer model that was being advertised in an hour-long infomercial with the blonde model who vacuums her house in a mini-skirt and candy apple red high heels?

Our society runs on capitalism. Therefore, it wants you to continuously throw out anything they deem obsolete, even if the previous model does a perfectly good job of doing what it's supposed to do. Go against the system. Rebel against the marketers. Don't be fooled into thinking that you need the latest Cuisinart that they are advertising. Trust me; you can still grate potatoes by hand. You can still make do with your old television. You don't need to run out and buy the latest gadget. You work hard for the money you have! Don't give it away!

Repolish and it's New Again

In keeping with the theme that you can make do with the older things in your home, I want to introduce another theme that is also conveniently forgotten in our "out with the old, in with the new" world. You can make most things that are old look new again. I have taken my older car to the car wash many times and have sat and watched while the workers clean and polish the vehicle inside and out. When they finish, and I walk up to the vehicle to retrieve it, I am always amazed at how new it looks. It looks and smells like a new car! This goes to show that anything that is older can be made to look new again with some dusting and cleaning.

I have ironed shirts that are many years old, and when I am finished with them, they look like new shirts again. You may want to go and inspect the furniture in your home. Just when you feel that you need to replace some furniture in your home, you may want to ask yourself whether it really needs to be replaced or whether it just could use another coat of paint or some furniture polish and some elbow grease. One of the tables in my room was purchased before I was born. I took the time to keep it polished and took good care of it. It looks new. You would never know how old it is just by looking at it. I mentioned in an earlier chapter the young man I knew in graduate school who wore a thirty year old shirt, and it still looked new! That goes to show that you can buck the strong forces in our society that are trying so hard to convince you that you need to buy the latest and newest. You don't.

Take one day that you are not working and try it. Take an older piece of furniture and polish it really well. More often than not, you will find that you can make it look new again, or at least newer. The same process can sometimes work for electronic appliances. Perhaps they are just a little dusty and can be made to look new again just by removing years' worth of grime off of them. It's worth the effort, and this process can be a source of fun for the whole family. You can separate the family into teams. One team can be in charge of polishing old furniture. Another team can be in charge of cleaning older appliances. Another team can be in charge of washing and ironing old clothing. And, even if after all that dusting, cleaning, ironing, and scrubbing, if your appliances and gadgets do show some signs of wear and tear, so be it. If they still work, then keep them. Don't junk them or donate them. Save your money!

USE LOW-COST HAIR PRODUCTS

Although this idea can be applied more easily to women, it also applies equally to men. Too often, our hair becomes another source of fret and spending. Countless shampoo ads are made that show a remarkable list of vitamins and proteins added to their shampoo formulas. Consider this – I once hear a hair expert saying that using a shampoo with vitamins is like rubbing vitamin enriched soil onto the leaves of a plant that is already above ground. Rubbing enriched soil does not do anything for the plant. It is the soil in which the plant is growing that is the most important element. It is what is beneath the ground that matters. Similarly, when it comes to your health, it is your nutrition level that matters, not what you put in your hair.

If you really like the fragrance of a certain shampoo, that's one thing. But, using a shampoo fortified with vitamins, minerals, and proteins is literally a waste of your money. All that is really necessary is to wash out the oils, dandruff, and grime that accumulate in human hair as a matter of course. However, the vitamins, minerals and proteins that are put into shampoos are a sham. They won't do a single thing for your hair. What the marketers are trying to do is to make you feel that you are taking greater care of your hair by washing it with a shampoo that is 'fortified' with vitamins and minerals. You're doing no such thing. You might as well rub a Vitamin C tablet on your hair, which won't do anything for your mane. However, what does make a huge difference for your hair is your diet. Only a well-balanced diet with plenty of protein can keep your hair shiny and strong. But most people don't realize this. Most television viewers are suckered into believing that using a protein-fortified shampoo will help their hair. Only the protein that goes into your stomach can truly go into your hair.

And, don't forget that stress has an enormous effect on the body. I have noticed that when I am stressed out, my hair appears a little thinner. But, when I am relaxed, my hair appears a lot thicker and fuller. This difference may be due to the fact that I eat better when there is no stress in my life. The better nutrition may account for the thickening of my hair. Also, I take a high-end vitamin and mineral packet with my meals. They are extremely powerful. These supplements probably do more for my hair than any shampoo that I buy. Don't be fooled into giving up your money on fancy shampoos!

Plant a Garden

In our age of technology, one of the things that we may be overlooking is nature. Nature can provide us with more beauty than we can fathom. One of the ways that you can enjoy nature is to plant a garden. You don't need a lot of space. Even if you live in an apartment, you can still plant a garden. It is a truly wondrous thing indeed to grow a small garden. You can plant the very fruits and vegetables that you may want to consume right in your own backyard! Simply set aside an area where you would like to grow something and keep it segregated for that purpose. You may want to grow your own tomatoes, or potatoes, or any vegetable or fruit that strikes your fancy.

Growing your own fruits and vegetables can be a way to connect with nature. You may have to learn a little about the seasons to grow and the right time to grow some things, but, in the end, it's all worth it. It's a great way to literally dig your hands into the Earth. If you have never developed your Green Thumb, this may be the best time to try. Don't pay the high prices that the grocery stores are charging for produce! Grow it yourself! Think of how rewarding it will feel to grow and then consume that which you have grown yourself! It will add immeasurably to your sense of self-efficacy and self-reliance. In our age or technology, our sense of being able to grow something by hand has been lost. And yet, a vital part of our heritage has been lost.

Being able to grow something with your own two hands contains within it a sense of wonder, of the divine. This is something which the American pioneers knew deep inside, yet it is something that modern citizens no longer feel. We have become too used to going to the store and buying produce that someone else has grown. Yet, this may very well be where the future of our race may dwell. We must return to a sense of self-reliance. But in so doing, we can regain a kinship to the Earth, to nature, and, ultimately, to God. It is a wonderfully liberating feeling to know that you don't need to depend on modern markets for the produce that you consume. You can grow it in your own backyard or in your terrace. And, don't forget that produce grown by hand has a richer, fuller taste than the produce that is grown with pesticides, hormones, and wax. The produce you grow at home is going to be healthier because it will be truly organic and grown with care and love. You will be able to taste the love.

MAKE YOUR HOME A SPA

I have run across some very splashy and glossy ads for spas. They welcome people to come and spend some time at a place where they can listen to soft music, get massages, smell nice aromatherapy scents, and be catered to, hand and foot. Although I have been intrigued by these ads, I can't help but believe that you can recreate the environment of a spa right in your own home. First of all, pick a day, or even an afternoon, when you know you will have no obligations whatsoever. Turn off your computer. Turn off your cell phone. Turn off any electronic device that may interfere with your Home Spa experience. If you were to receive a phone call or a text to which you feel you must respond, it will take you out of the mental space or 'zone' to which you need to go in order to experience the full effect of your home spa.

Find some soft instrumental music that you can play in your home. Take a day when you don't work and allow yourself to wander around your home *au naturale*! Wear a terry cloth robe and simply allow yourself to lounge in your home. Pick some very light organic foods to eat and don't eat a lot. Light some small tea light candles in your bathroom and fill your bathtub with warm water. Place a couple of tea lights at the corners at the far end of your tub, on opposite sides of your feet. Bring your CD player or radio into your bathroom and play the softest music you can find. Turn the lights off and just allow the candles to be the only light you have in your bathroom.

I know someone who has a ritual for days when she is stressed out. She turns off all the lights in her bathroom and takes a shower in the dark. You may want to do this or take a long, indulgent bath by candle light. After your bath, rub some natural oil all over your skin and then wrap yourself up in your favorite bathrobe. Then go to your bed where you can cuddle up and fall gently asleep. You may want to add some variety for your at-home spa routine. Have your spouse, or partner, or even your friend give you a vigorous back massage. Have your partner massage your legs and feet. Continue to play some soft, mellow music of your choice. You may want to indulge in foods that you normally don't have, like some chocolates, or a very full-flavored red wine. Spend some time meditating or praying. The point is to make your home spa a place where you can get away from it all. But, you will be saving yourself hundreds of dollars!

Take a Vacation at Home

One of the things that I have noticed while living in Southern California is the number of people who all leave, at the same time, on national holidays. Not only do they all congregate on the freeways, but they also pack the airports as well. Try spending your vacation at home. You will save yourself not only hundreds of dollars, but you will also save yourself all of the stress and headaches of going on a vacation and finding out that everyone and their cousin also had the same idea. I have personally seen airports being jammed-packed with people, even on regular weekends! I can only imagine what they must look like two days before Thanksgiving or Christmas. People may complain about the stress in our culture, but I firmly believe that much of the stress that people complain about is self-induced. That is to say, they are creating that stress for themselves.

I can't help but think of the character of Neil Page in the movie *Planes, Trains, and Automobiles*. Imagine all the stress he would have saved himself had he simply told his wife that he would not be able to make it home on time for Thanksgiving. Would it really have been the end of the world? Even the first Pilgrims who celebrated the first Thanksgiving were not celebrating it with their extended family. Their extended families were still in England. People create their own stress just because our culture has told them that they must be together with their families on Thanksgiving or Christmas. Don't fall for this message. Avoid the airports and freeways on Memorial Day and other such holidays. Spend it at home, making a leisurely barbecue in the backyard with the family pet.

People willingly create their own stress by acting in a compulsive way at certain times of the year. Why? Just to fulfill some national collective consciousness? Save your car wear and tear by keeping it at home during the holiday season. Don't put your pet in a kennel or dump your children with a sitter. Spend time with your family at home and enjoy the fruits of your labor and the joy of being able to truly relax. I heard recently that countless Americans are at work, dreaming of a vacation. But, when they are on vacation, they are stressing out about the work that awaits them when they return to the office. They are wasting vacation time and thousands of dollars by not truly being in the moment during their vacation. Do yourself a favor, take a vacation at home. Make it fun!

TAKE A MENTAL VACATION

If you are too busy to take an actual vacation, take a mental vacation. Close your eyes and picture yourself on a beach with a cool drink in your hand. Listen to the soft sounds of the mellow waves as they crash lazily against the shore. The fun part of taking a mental vacation is that you can design it to be any way you want it to be! You can be in a gondola in Venice, being rowed down the rows of old building and churches. Or, you can be in the Swiss Alps, racing down a slope on your own set of skis. Get wild and crazy in your imagination. Do something in your mind that you may not feel comfortable doing in real life. Perhaps you may want to imagine what it's like to be in a diving cage and come face to face with great white sharks! Or, you can be on an African safari and imagine what it's like to look outside of your jeep and see lions roaming free. Or, you can jump out of a plane and go skydiving!

The fun part of taking a mental vacation is that you can take one whenever you want, and you can make it last as long as you like! If you're at work, you can take a one-minute vacation and allow yourself to sunbathe in Fiji. After the minute has passed, you can then return to your work. Although it may not be quite the same as taking an actual vacation, taking a mental vacation can be a quick pick-me-up in the middle of a hectic day. You can control the action and the setting. It's like being able to be the director of your own movie. Only the movie will be strictly your own, and it will be played in the movie theater of your mind.

If you're the type of individual who likes to take naps, you may want to incorporate this as part of your nap routine. Simply lie down and imagine yourself in the middle of a forest, or ocean, or sand dunes, or whatever place you want to imagine. Basically, what you will be doing is to practice a form of meditation. The art of meditation entails the practice of emptying the mind of all its worldly cares and anxieties. The next step in meditation is to allow the mind to remain empty or to allow it to enjoy peaceful guided imagery or a mantra. Try it during a busy day. Allow yourself a one-minute mental vacation. As a result of doing this, you may find yourself not needing to take as many actual vacations or to get away as often as you were used to doing. Mental vacations are free, fun, and can be taken almost as often as you like. You can go anywhere in time – past, present, or the future. Try it!

HAVE A MOVIE NIGHT AT HOME

As a child and adolescent, I think that there have been few experiences as fun as going to the movies. I loved the smell of the fresh popcorn filling every nook and cranny of the movie theater. I loved seeing all of the goodies being sold at the concession stand. It was like entering Movie Heaven. And, whenever I do go to the movies as an adult, I am still taken aback by all of these same sensory experiences. However, with the price of movie tickets rising so steadily, and with the dearth of good movies being made, I have now made it a habit to enjoy movie nights at home. I buy good quality popcorn, and put plenty of butter on it. I also buy Goobers and Junior Mints. I lower the lighting in my living room, and, presto! I have my own miniature movie theater at home.

It's great fun to enjoy movies at home. You can select the movies you want to watch and you can control the sound. In this day and age, fewer and fewer people are able to afford to go to the movies. The prices of movie tickets, even at the matinee price, have become too expensive for the average working-class family to afford. A family of two adults and two small children may end up spending close to one hundred dollars for one movie! First of all, they have to purchase the movie tickets. If they go in the evening, they have to pay more per ticket. The price of a large popcorn, plus four sodas and candy all add up to a lot of money. They may even have to pay for parking on top of that. If the children want to go to McDonald's either before or after, that only raises the cost even more.

If you are among the countless Americans who are looking for ways to cut back on costs, then try watching movies at home. Invite friends over to your home. If the movie watching is among adults, you may want to serve some wine, or other adult refreshments. Make it as fun as you want. Watch scary movies on Halloween. Watch sentimental favorites on Christmas. Watch history movies on Thanksgiving. If you have small children, you'll be setting a good example for them. Show them that there are ways to enjoy life without spending a lot of money. Our culture has convinced us that in order to enjoy some forms of entertainment that there is only 'one' correct way of doing it. Go against the grain. You don't have to spend your money to enjoy a movie night at home. All you need to do is to turn off the lights, get some tasty snacks and pop the movie into the DVD player!

SPEND TIME WITH YOUR FAMILY

In this day and age, countless families are living fragmented lives. It seems as though fewer and fewer families are spending quality time together. On some level, part of the problem has been the invasion of technology into our homes. Kids eat dinner in front of the computer. Or, they eat it in front of the television. Meals are no longer a time when families can come together and truly commune. Even trips in the family van are no longer what they used to be. Rather than talk, children sit in the back seat watching the television set that swings down from the top console, or they have their own individual television monitors situated on the backs of the front seats. They sit glued watching the screens like zombies.

Young people are taking advantage of technology to tune out the world around them, and as a result of this, they are losing their ability to relate to the world around them, and to the people around them. If you have children living with you at home, try to set aside time each day, perhaps at dinner time, when no electronic device will be allowed to be used, and devote that time for quality interaction. Ask each other about the accomplishments of the day. Find out how everyone is doing. Find out how your children are doing in school. Ask them about their day. Encourage them to talk. And encourage them to elaborate rather than give the usual one-word answer, "It's fine." The current weakened state of the economy can become a new time when families can renew their ties to one another, and to take stock of what is, and what is not, important in life.

Make dinner a time to reconnect, to toss out the stressors of the day and to feel the love and warmth of home. It doesn't matter what is being served for dinner. What matters is that quality time is spent with loved ones. The grand irony about today's technology is that it is supposed to connect people to one another, and yet, it is doing exactly the opposite. It is causing people to tune out the actual flesh and blood people around them. How is technology connecting us to other people when we are not even aware of the people who are actually sitting in front of us? So take time each day to tell the important people in your life that you love them. Let them know how important they are to you. Express your gratitude to them for all that they have done for you. Let them know you care about them, and that they matter to you. Give it a try.

SPEND TIME WITH PETS

Pets can be a wonderful way to connect to nature. They are simple-minded and they are cute. It seems that so many pets have a personality all their own. Some are playful all the time, and others are more curious about their world, and constantly sniffing their world. Some modern research has shown that the presence of a pet can be a wonderful way to boost your immune system. It seems that there is a special bond between humans and their pets. This relationship, as such, is indescribable, really. It's as though they intuitively understand us, and are in tune with how we are feeling. If you live in a house, and don't currently own a pet, you may want to consider bringing a little friend home one day. Some people are ardent cat lovers.

Sometimes I am tempted to generalize and state that women prefer cats, and that men prefer dogs, and yet I know that this is not always the case. There are plenty of women who truly enjoy the company of their dogs. You can see many of these women walking their dogs in the suburbs of Los Angeles. I suppose that many women feel protected by their dog, particularly if he is of a larger size. (I suppose that a Chihuahua is not really going to help a woman feel safer) Many men enjoy having cats in their home and feel a certain kinship to them. Therefore, there is a wide variety of preferences in the type of pet that people enjoy having in their homes. A bird can be a wonderful way of enlivening a house or backyard. You may want to consider going to a pet shop and browsing around at the different types of pets that they offer. Some people are completely satisfied by having a couple of gold fish in a tank.

Pets can offer a type of companionship that can fill a void, particularly if you don't have any other person living in your home. And, some pets, particularly the larger dogs, can allow a person to sleep better at night and feel protected from strangers. It is true that caring for a pet involves much time, effort and money. However, if you are the type of individual that enjoys animals, you may find the labor involved in owning a pet to be a labor of love. Countless people enjoy having their pet jump onto their beds in the morning and snuggle with their owners. The feel of a little fury friend next to you, one that breathes and barks or purrs, is a truly wonderful experience. They can help you feel that the world is not always a terrible place. They remind you that there truly is joy in giving love.

TRY NEW FOODS

One way of breaking up the doldrums of modern life is to switch things around in your home in order to experience some badly needed novelty. One way that I have done this is to alter my menus. I have found it a wonderful experience to look at my shopping cart in the grocery store, and then having to look at it twice, as the food items in the cart are hardly recognizable. It almost seems as though it was someone else's cart. The reason was that I was putting unfamiliar foods in the shopping cart. I enjoy trying different fruit juices, and other beverages, such as soy milk. There are organic foods that you can try, and imported foods as well.

The fun part about food is that it allows you to travel around the world! Try some hummus or some matzo, and you can be in the Middle East! Try some fresh basil and oregano and sprinkle it on some pasta and you're now in a far off village in Italy! Mix together some peanut butter and some other ingredients, and you can make a wonderful Thai Peanut Sauce for your noodles or main dish. Food allows us to get to know other cultures, at least on a culinary level. Food allows us to understand the values and the heritage that people in other parts of the world have claimed as their own.

Some scholars have claimed that it is the universal language of love, or of mathematics, or of music that binds people from diverse parts of the world together. However, food certainly plays a large part in uniting diverse peoples together in a common mission of enjoying good food. The act of trying new cuisine, particular ethnic cuisine, transcends language, and it actually transcends other cultural barriers as well, such as religion. It has been said to countless women through the ages that the quickest route to a man's heart is through his stomach.

That may be true, but it is also true that the quickest way to travel to a far-flung destination, indeed to travel, even if it is only in your mind, is to embrace the cuisine of different cultures throughout the world. This doesn't mean that you have to try foods that seem thoroughly disgusting or that you just could not stomach. I consider myself quite open minded and even I have my limitations! However, by keeping as open a mind as possible, and by being as daring and as adventurous as possible, you may find that the cultures of the world may come knocking at your door. Or, at least, they may come knocking on the door of your refrigerator!

Hold a Garage Sale

A garage sale may be a great way to get rid of a lot of clutter and dead weight that has accumulated in your home. Garage sales are an excellent way to get rid of things that you don't want or don't need any more. However, as opposed to giving things away to the local Salvation Army or Goodwill, garage sales represent one final attempt at making a little money from the things that you own. What you may consider doing is to go through your house, room by room, and try to find as many things as possible that you no longer use, or need, or want, anymore. Garage sales are also a wonderful opportunity to find things that you may want at very reasonable prices. I have acquired some very nice items at garage sales, and the prices were quite reasonable. Garage sales are a venue where you can put your haggling skills to good use.

Nevertheless, the main purpose of a garage sale is to get rid of clutter that no longer has any usefulness for you. By going from room to room and taking stock of all the things that no longer have any use or no longer have any appeal to you, the greater the inventory that you can have at your next garage sale. Part of the appeal of garage sales is that they allow you to recover at least some of the value that you invested in purchasing an item. For example, if you purchased a Cuisinart five years ago, but have only used it once, or not at all, then a garage sale allows you to recover at least some of the money you paid to acquire the Cuisinart. And, garage sales need not be a whole-day affair. Post some signs around town that you are having a garage sale and post the address. Then, do your best to neatly display your wares on your front lawn.

Garage sales attract more attention than you may realize. Plus, you may have the chance at getting to know some of your neighbors, people that you may not have otherwise been in contact with had you not had the garage sale. Hold the garage sale until around noon. At that point, cut your losses and count how much money you made. At that point, you may want to reward yourself, or your family, by ordering a pizza and celebrating the sales which took place. Garage sales are a way to make money on the side while not feeling pressured, the way one would feel in a regular job. Garage sales allow you to let go of items that were holding you down. In a lean economy, being able to supplement your income is valuable. You may even make some friends in the process.

Category III

Nutrition and Health

GIVE UP THE JUNK FOOD

If you are planning a new way of life, one based upon real needs, rather than culturally-imposed excesses, one good idea may be to cut junk food out of your life. If your wish is to curb your spending, and to begin living a life based upon simplicity and being close to God, then one way to create a healthier lifestyle for yourself is to cut out the bad types of food for your system. Supermarkets are jammed packed with foods that have close to zero nutritional value and have lots of calories but no nutrients. Do your body a favor. Buy only wholesome, natural foods. Purchase only foods that provide essential nutrients. Why would you want to give your body anything other than what it needs? I have personally found it rewarding to eat natural foods and to feel that I am returning to the Earth, as it were.

Natural foods are alive, and they impart their lives to us. Processed as well as sugar- and salt-laden foods wreak havoc on the body. They contribute nothing to the immune system. Start by purchasing more fruits and vegetables at the grocery store. Start with the ones you like. Perhaps you may have a hankering for spinach. Or, perhaps you might really enjoy some broccoli. Become creative. Make some creamed spinach or some creamed corn. The point is, if your budget is slim, don't purchase foods are bad for your body. Instead, buy the foods that are life-affirming. If you have a family, don't feed them junk food. Give them only the foods that allow the human body to operate at its maximum. Provide them foods which supply the nutrients which allow the immune system to function at full gallop.

Fortunately, the Internet provides us with all the information we need regarding essential nutrients as well as vitamins and minerals. Take some time to learn about the different nutrients the body requires at each stage during its lifespan. This information is free. Make use of it. People take health for granted. By eliminating junk food from your life, you will be streamlining your life and only including the things that add value, or health, to your life and getting rid of unhealthy habits, such as eating junk food. Any walk through a modern grocery store reveals the amount of junk food that we put into our bodies. It's no wonder that people get cancer. A treat once in a while is all right, but try to keep to a diet that is as natural as possible. Your outlook on health will change, and your body will thank you.

Design Creative Menus

One of the ideas that I recently developed was that of having creative menus during the week. This can be particularly fun if you have a family of picky eaters. For instance, you can create the menus around certain themes. I have noticed that what has made certain theme parks so much fun is the extent to which they carry their diverse and fun themes into every nook and cranny. One of the ways that they do this so creatively is with their menus. Breakfast, lunch, and dinner are offered on menus that have been given creative names. Why not carry this idea into your home. This will be big hit if you have small children, but I think even teenagers will get a kick out of it. You may want to sit down with a piece of paper and a pen, and think of different themes and types of cuisine that you may want to create, such as: Meatball Mondays, Tortellini Tuesdays, Western Wednesdays, Thick-Soup Thursdays, Frijoles Fridays, Swashbuckling Saturdays, and Sun-Baked Sundays.

Use your computer and design menus ahead of time, using the themes created for the days of the week. For example, with Meatball Mondays, create a menu that has outer space themes on it, showing meatballs raining down like meteors, etc. Then, in the menu, you can continue the creativity with fun-sounding names, such as Meteor Meatball Sandwiches, and serve them hot with tomato sauce. Or, serve them up with Launch Linguini, or Space Spaghetti, and so on. On Tortellini Tuesdays, design a menu with an Italian theme. Find photos of the Leaning Tower of Pisa or other iconic images of Italy and put them on the menu.

You may even want to find some festive Italian music and play it softly in the background as you serve and enjoy dinner. Western Wednesdays are meant for a Wild West showdown dinner! Serve up a menu with barbecue sauce, corn on the cob, chili, and corn bread, and print the menus with Old West fonts. Play some country music in the background, just for fun. Thick Soup Thursdays can be an evening for Clam Chowder, or Corn Chowder, or any thick soup. Frijoles Fridays can be a South-of-the-Border fiesta with spicy enchiladas, tacos, burritos, or whatever may appeal to your family's palates. Swashbuckling Saturdays can have a pirate theme. Serve non-alcoholic grog and some fresh steamed or grilled seafood. Make eating an adventure and a way to travel in time and to different places.

GIVE HERBAL REMEDIES A CHANCE

In this day and age, with health care a subject of such intense debate, it may be a wise idea to keep your options open when it comes to your family's health. Today's world still has many pathogens and contagions, so it is just as important as ever to safeguard your health and that of your family. To that end, there are many herbal and natural remedies that are available and are purported to cure a host of ailments. The next time someone in your family is ill, or comes down with a strange malady or exotic ailment, look up some of the more natural remedies that are available. I have personally tried a range of remedies and the results were mixed. Some worked more than others. However, we all have different body chemistries and different tolerances to certain substances, so try to be as aware as possible of what your body needs. Talk to your physician as a first step. If you are not satisfied with the advice or medicine you are prescribed, then turn to the more natural remedies that are available.

As with any endeavor, be aware of the charlatans and the snake oil vendors. I once heard a physician give a guest talk at a college. He works in an office that has predominantly Latino patients. Many of these people practice more natural forms of healing, but, he told us that many times his patients will come in complaining of an ailment, and, when asked what they take for the pain, they produce a bag of essentially, grass! It was probably collected by the gardener, placed in a plastic bag, and sold as a miracle cure drug! There have always been, and always will be, people anxious and ready to take your money.

It has been unfortunate that the debate over the use of traditional Western medicine versus the use natural homeopathic remedies has caused people to go to their respective corners of the ring, rather than to come to some agreement and find a middle ground. It reminds me of the debate of Creationism versus Evolution. People, it seems, go to one end of the debate or the other. Try to maintain a flexible state of mind. It needn't be either entirely one way or the other. Keep a fluid approach to life. Use the best that traditional Western medicine has to offer. Then use the best that natural remedies have to offer. Just be sure that whatever natural remedy you are using doesn't interfere with the traditional medicine you are taking. The best compromise lies in having a balanced approach between West and East.

BROWN BAG YOUR LUNCH

It is truly amazing to see the amount of money that people spend on their morning cup of coffee, and then on their lunch breaks. Starbucks has been notorious for charging exorbitant prices for a cup of Java. Don't give them your money! There are plenty of delicious brews available in the grocery stores. When it comes to having lunch at work, merely engage in a little menu planning the night before. It will cost you much less money to take a lunch to work than it will to buy a meal during your lunch break. What most people don't do, when trying to figure out how to spend less money, is they forget to annualize the costs involved.

Let's assume that you and your coworkers enjoy going to a nice Mexican restaurant during your lunch break. Let's further assume that each platter costs $13.00, which is conservative. You will probably want a drink with the meal. Add another $4.00 dollars. That's $17.00 for lunch, minus tax. Add the tax and it comes close to $20.00! Just one meal! Five days a week comes to $100 dollars in just one work week, plus the gas during the commute to get to the restaurant. Imagine that. Now, here comes the hard part. Annualize the cost. Let's imagine that you work 50 weeks a year (assuming you take off two weeks for vacation or illness, or both). Now let's do the math: 50 multiplied by 20. That's a thousand dollars a year in lunches out with your coworkers! Is it worth it? You must ask yourself that very difficult question.

Imagine that your boss came up to you and said, "I would like to give you a thousand dollar bonus at the end of the year." You would most likely jump for joy! The condition for the bonus? Take ten minutes each night and put together a menu for the next day and take your lunch with you to work. That's all. I realize that lunch out is not just about the food. It's about breaking bread with friends and coworkers. I can understand that. Perhaps you can design a set of fun activities that does not involve spending money, such as planning a day at the beach or the lake. Everyone can bring his or her own lunch. Perhaps you may want to design a movie night at your home. All you might want to provide is the popcorn, and drinks. And, yet, you can elect several of the guests to bring the snacks. The point is, you don't have to spend money when you socialize. You can spend time with people without spending money. All it takes is the will and creativity. That's all it takes.

DON'T PURCHASE COOKBOOKS!

In the past, one of the tools of the trade that any "dutiful" wife and house-maker would have is a good cookbook. It was *de riguer*. Now, with the rules of cooking and cleaning having become more equitable between men and women, and with the Internet being such a mainstay in our world, the older notion of a cookbook being part of a dowry is a thing of the past. You no longer have to buy Betty Crocker's cookbook in order to cook dinner for your family. Now, all you have to do is go online and download a recipe. What I have done is to create a file on my computer with the recipes that I have found while looking for chcap and low-cost recipes. This is where the Internet really is a gift and a blessing. There are literally thousands of recipes that can be found on-line. And, best of all, they're free!

People have taken the time to share their 'secret recipes' online, so take advantage of that! You don't need to buy a cookbook. You may still want to have a good working printer so that you can print out the recipe you're going to follow for dinner. What you may want to do, instead of purchasing a cookbook, is to create your own cookbook! Simply print out all of the recipes that you collect over time, and place them neatly in a notebook. Or you can be creative and make it a scrapbook. Place pictures of the finished recipes next to the recipes themselves. You may want to scribble your own comments. I have personally cooked many things, all the while faithfully copying someone else's recipe. Yet, I have found, time and again, that the recipe which someone else wrote down doesn't quite seem or taste the way I want it to, so I either write down or make a mental note to change the recipe.

The wonderful thing about recipes is that, like music, or the 26 letters of the alphabet, there is a near infinite amount of creativity or variations that can be accomplished. All it takes is a little ingenuity and elbow grease, or should I say olive oil? Take note of which meals you cook the most. See if you can find other variations for the recipe, just to change things up a bit. Take a while and sit down at your computer and do an on-line search for recipes. You may be quite surprised and pleased with the world of recipes that you will discover. If you are trying to keep your food budget within certain bounds, then do Google searches for cheap or easy-to-make recipes. Both you and your family will love the universe of recipes out there!

TRY NEW ETHNIC FOODS

One of the most rewarding benefits of trying new and different foods over the years is being able to travel through foods. Food allows us to discover our world. It allows us to travel beyond our immediate vicinity. It allows us to broaden our borders and our boundaries. Through food, I have managed to travel, at least in a culinary sense, to India, Italy, China, Japan, Mexico, Russia, Scotland, and Southern states of our Union. Food allows our palates to wander the world. It has been said that there are some 'languages' that are universal, such as the universal language of mathematics, or of music, or love. That may be true, but there is also the universal language of food. Culinary pleasures are truly universal. While doing a Google search for recipes, as I recommended in the previous example, I also recommend looking for exotic recipes.

Try looking for something that is outside your comfort zone. And, remember, when you cook at home, you have much more control over the process and the ingredients. Therefore, you need not go through the anxieties that are attendant upon the usual travel or vacation experience, whereupon, you may not be entirely aware of how fresh the food is, or whether it was rinsed with clean water, or whether it is stale. I have gotten sick from the food in Mexico and it was a painful experience indeed. But, at home, you have a lot more control over the experience. You get to control the amount of spices and other 'exotic' ingredients are placed into the food. It can be fun to also study the history of food. Some of the recipes that people take for granted have some very interesting stories behind them.

I once heard someone tell me that the Earl of Sandwich, in England, was so engrossed in his gambling and card games, that he simply ordered someone to just throw some meat between two slices of bread to keep him fed during his games. This is where the sandwich was born. I don't know if this is true. I would not doubt it. Therefore, allow your kitchen to be your new atlas, and let it take you around the world! Let one night be devoted to European cuisine, and another night to be devoted to Asian cuisine. And, don't forget the cuisine that lies in our oceans as well. Shark meat can be quite tasty, as can squid. Our earth has given us unique ingredients. Put them together in a fashion that is as worldly as possible. While actual travel is not always possible, it is always possible through food.

LET NATURE BE YOUR GYM

Nature can and does provide us with wonderful ways to get in shape. I have found that a long walk on a beach can be great way to tone up and get some fresh air, all the while enjoying the majesty and beauty of the ocean. Forests can provide us with paths and trails that require only a good pair of walking shoes and the will to get in shape. Plus, nature provides us with the most panoramic and beautiful vistas imaginable. I think that children know this inherently better than adults. It's not uncommon to find children climbing trees and swimming in the ocean for hours. But, as responsible, educated adults, we take the high road and go to modern gyms, with their modern equipment and sterilized atmosphere. There is nothing wrong with this approach.

If you are already a member of a gym and find that it works well for you, then continue using it. All I am recommending here is that you consider using other, less 'traditional' forms of getting exercise. Swimming in the ocean or a lake is a great way to get in shape. And, if you are land-locked, and a lake or ocean is too far to be a practical locale in which to exercise, then consider taking a friendly stroll down your neighborhood block. At the very least, you are exposed to the (relatively) clean air, and you can perhaps take your partner or friend with you. Power walks have become a very popular way to keep in shape. You can even take a power walk on your lunch break!

The human body is not designed to be inside of office buildings for eight hours every day, sitting on stiff chairs and breathing recycled air. We were meant to be outside, in the fresh air. That is our heritage. However, now that we are no longer living in caves and hunting wooly mammoths, we have to adapt ourselves to our modern world. Of course, with this development have come many benefits as well, such as modern medicine. However, my concern is that we, as a species, have lost touch with nature.

I grew up not far from the ocean, and so the water quickly became the area that I most associated with peace and tranquility. I still find myself transfixed by the sight of the ocean. I go to the water as often as possible. But, what I have come to value as part of my excursions to the water is the opportunity to walk from one end of the beach to the other. All told, it's a pretty long walk. And, I get to enjoy the smell of the saline air, and the ocean mist. It is a true joy to be able to utilize the 'natural' gymnasium that God created for us.

CATEGORY IV

Lifestyle

Slow Down

One of the simplest, yet, in a philosophical sense, one of the most profound things I have done in my recent years is to learn to slow down. We live in a society where "time is money." That statement speaks volumes about our culture! It has placed upon our collective consciousness a pressure to achieve as much as possible and to not waste a single minute. This is the fast track to a heart attack. We have become a culture so obsessed with time, and with not wasting time, that we pay people, known as efficiency experts, good money for their expertise on how a company or corporate entity can operate faster, or more smoothly.

Earlier in the book I mentioned the instance when I was at the car wash, enjoying the soft summer breeze, and allowed myself a moment to relax and close my eyes and take a ten-minute break. The young woman next to me sat down and was texting like a madwoman, and never once stopped to slow down and enjoy the day or the weather. This is disconcerting, because it says a lot about our culture. We do not take the time to put our iPhone and laptops away and just enjoy the moment. People take their laptops on vacation. They use them during their airplane flights. They use them at restaurants. They never slow down. Why? Do they feel guilty if they slow down? Do they feel that they are wasting time if they were to just concentrate on the food they were eating? Do they consider such enjoyments evidence of laziness? People should slow down. They will find themselves old and worn out, and wondering what they ever did in life besides work.

I believe that we live in a culture that is constantly pressing the fast-forward button. I am domiciled in Southern California, and I am therefore routinely forced to drive on the freeways to get from one city to another. It never ceases to amaze me to see the angry, aggressive drivers. I once waited an extra six or eight seconds to let a bicycle rider cross an intersection before getting onto a freeway on-ramp. The woman behind me was having a cow, and when I made my right turn onto the freeway, she sped ahead of me on the lane next to me, and turned around to look at me. She was yelling at me inside of her car. And, sadly, this has become the norm in our culture. Take time to slow down. Do your work, and do it efficiently, but do allow yourself the time to enjoy a summer breeze. Life is much shorter than you realize. Enjoy it while you're alive.

UNPLUG YOUR iPHONE, iPAD, AND LAPTOP

One of the ways that you can slow and enjoy more out of life is to unplug yourself from all of the electronic gadgetry that we have become accustomed to in our daily lives. Our iPhones, iPads, Kindle Readers, lap top computer, and regular cell phones have taken over our every free moment. As I mentioned in the previous section, I see people plugged into their gadgetry at restaurants, on airplanes, and even at the movies. If people are going to be using their laptops at the movies, then why bother going to the movies in the first place? Why bother paying twelve dollars per ticket, only to be using the laptop the entire time? They might as well save themselves the twelve dollars, as well as the drive, and paying for parking, and just stay home.

It seems that there is a keen uneasiness in people about unplugging from their computerized world. It's as if they feel uncomfortable with the thought of one or two free hours. And, yet, the supreme irony it is not as though they are even doing important work on their computers. More likely than not, they are on Facebook! It's not as though they are about to close a one hundred thousand dollar deal for their company or for themselves. Perhaps I might be more sympathetic in those instances.

I suppose that it is, in the end, a fear of wasting time that these people exhibit. But isn't what they are doing on Facebook a leisure activity, ergo, a waste of time? It certainly isn't work! I have even heard of people who take their laptops to the beach! It seems that people have lost touch with the practice of truly emptying their minds, in a Zen sort of way, for example, being at one with the waves at the beach, or at one with the trees in the park, or the flowers in the garden. People have developed hyperactive minds that don't allow them to relax, even in settings that encourage relaxation. It's a pity, really.

It is a sad statement about our culture that we have forgotten how to do nothing. Just to sit, or lie down, and....relax. It costs nothing. It is a free activity. My recommendation is that you try the approach used by behavioral psychologists when they try to change a client's behavior – do it in stages. Try shutting off your cell phone for an hour. Then try two hours. Then try three hours. More likely than not, you'll likely notice that nothing catastrophic happened to you. Then try unplugging yourself from your iPad for an hour, then two hours, and so on. Give it a try.

ENJOY THE ULTIMATE FREEBIE—SEX

In our plugged-in electronic world, it's important to separate ourselves from the madness of constant mindless texting and to feel that we can connect in a deep and profound way with another individual. One of the most important ways to be able to do this is through a sexual relationship with a partner, or spouse. In connecting to another individual on a sexual level, we are able to feel a deep emotional and spiritual connection to another individual. God gave us a natural sexuality for a reason. It is up to us to honor and cherish this natural appetite and to enjoy it with another person.

There are few experiences as profound as being able to express ones love to another person physically. In consummating the act of love, one is able to feel a profound vulnerability and yet, a unparalleled connection to another human being. The experience of physical love connects us to the eternal. One author once went so far as to state that, at the height of the sexual act, one is brought into contact with God, or the Universal. It is the ultimate letting go. It is the stuff of poets and psychoanalysts. And, yet, they are correct in exalting the act of sex as one which takes us to a state of absolute *nirvana* and back. (Talk about a natural high!)

Sex is what even keeps couples in lousy marriages together. It can have a rather addictive quality. That is why it is so important to have the right partner or spouse with which to enjoy it. It is also a wonderful way to relieve stress! What better way to spend a rainy afternoon or a snowed-in day than to have a rendezvous with your loved one! In a world where people are searching for ways to enjoy life without spending money, this has to be at the top of everyone's list. The only expense involved would be the little extras that people sometimes acquire in order to enhance the romantic aspect of being with a partner, such as roses, or a nice perfume or cologne.

Partners can also invest in slinky or silky outfits that are designed to entice their partners. Those are understandable purchases, as they represent an investment in the relationship. A purchase which is an investment for the maintenance or even the betterment of the relationship is never an unwise choice, as long as the spending remains within reasonable limits. Even discount stores such as Kmart and Walmart have their 'evening wear' sections, so you needn't spend a lot of money to take home an outfit which is sure to light a fire in the bedroom! Enjoy!

ENJOY FREE MUSIC

One of the activities that our parents and grandparents enjoyed, and enjoyed it immensely, was the act of listening to the radio. The radio represented the world, and it was brought right into people's living rooms. People would listen to the radio for hours and that was the main form of entertainment for countless individuals. It was only later that the idea of "purchasing" music on vinyl records later took hold. The idea still holds sway for many people. For some people, the idea of owning music that they can play over and over again has taken on a life of its own.

Someone once told me that modern music storage devices can hold thousands of songs in their memories. I don't think that I even know more than two hundred songs, and even that number is a stretch! When I was growing up, the usage of compact cassettes was in full swing. Later, compact discs were all the rage, and everyone ran out to buy CDs. Now, songs are downloaded digitally from the Internet and stored in a computer's memory and listened to on digital storage devices. It seems that the lowly radio has been all but forgotten.

Yet, there is no reason that a radio cannot be enjoyed these days. It seems that people must feel that they must 'own' something in order to enjoy it. The music industry has made a lot of money by pandering to people's proprietary tendencies with music. After buying the CD, the music is yours to keep. Yet, music belongs to humanity. It does not really belong to anyone in particular. The only people who have exclusive legal rights to songs are the music distribution companies, or the music labels that sell and promote musical artists.

Listening to the radio can be an adventure. As Forrest Gump might say about listening to the radio: "You never know what you're gonna get." Indeed, the songs are different one to the next, but that's what makes listening to the radio such fun. They may play one of your favorite songs, but they may also play songs you may have never heard before. Give it a try. Radios are still sold in stores, believe it or not. They're fun to take to the beach or to the park for a picnic. Radios also serve other purposes. They are handy to have in an emergency. The Emergency Broadcast Service will use the airwaves to inform people of what they must do to stay safe in an emergency. Nevertheless, give radio a try. The music on the radio is free and it represents the adventure of not knowing what lies ahead!

Drive Slower, and Enjoy the Drive

Save money by treating your vehicle well. One of the techniques that can accomplish this is to slow down when you drive. Driving fast not only burns more gasoline, but it also produces more wear and tear on your automobile. The engine is forced to run faster than its optimum speed. This is what causes cars to burn more gasoline. With the price of gas once again inching higher, it may be a good idea to slow down and not burn gasoline so quickly. But there is another benefit to this as well. By slowing down when you drive, you are also saving wear and tear on yourself.

I drive in Southern California nearly every day. And, I am always taken aback by the number of people who drive like maniacs on the road. They speed, tailgate, and weave in and out through traffic. As the years pass by and as I keep learning to take life a little more slowly, I am always amazed at the self-imposed stress that these people impose on themselves. They think nothing of wearing themselves and their vehicles out. Not only are they paying more for vehicle upkeep and maintenance, but they are also going to be paying a much larger price in terms of heart conditions, ulcers, and other stress-related diseases.

Do yourself and your car a favor. Slow down and enjoy the drive. Let the other crazies crash and kill themselves! You don't have to drive like they do. Every single time that I have seen two or more vehicles off to the side of the road, or on the shoulder of the freeway, it almost never fails that one of the two vehicles was tailgating the other. In other words, the driver at fault was driving aggressively. Time and again. It is amazing to see how often it happens. Don't be the next statistic. Do not drive aggressively or tailgate. You will end up ruining your vehicle and your health. It's not worth it. Instead, put on the radio and enjoy some free music.

If you drive very fast because you have to get to work on time, then get up earlier. If getting up earlier is a problem, then go to bed earlier. It's that simple. People allow themselves to be stressed out unnecessarily. It really can be as simple as the decision to go to bed earlier and then getting up the next day, refreshed and rested. This way, you can enjoy the ride to work or school, without the need to drive aggressively or to speed. You will save money by needing less upkeep and maintenance on your vehicle. You will also save money by not having to go to the doctor to treat your ulcer!

In my years of teaching, I have counseled many students on this point. When they were taking my psychology classes, I was reminding them that romantic relationships are only one type of relationship. Yet, there are many categories of relationships; there are family relationships, work relationships, and friendships. Our entire lives are built around relationships. And, yet, they all require effort and a fair amount of investment and work. Therefore, when I recommend that people work on their relationships, I am recommending that they work on all of them, not just their romantic relationships. They all deserve our best foot forward, and our commitment.

GO FOR A WALK AFTER DINNER

Going for a walk after dinner can be a pleasurable way to stimulate your digestion while getting some fresh air. So many families have dinner and later congregate in front of the television. However, the effect of this lifestyle choice is that it can encourage a sedentary lifestyle. With so many children who are obese as a result of not getting enough exercise, a walk after dinner, while not technically qualifying as an aerobic or cardiovascular exercise, can nevertheless encourage a more active way of life. It can become an enjoyable family routine.

Right after dinner has ended, invite your family to join you for a walk. If you live alone, invite a friend or acquaintance to join you for a postprandial walk. Perhaps you may want to take your pet with you on your walk. Dogs really enjoy being taken out on walks in the evening. It's their chance to explore their world. Walking right after dinner or any other meal for that matter, allows you to gain energy from the meal, rather than allowing you to succumb to the ordinary sleepiness that meals may cause. The next time you finish dinner, simply put the dirty dishes in the sink, slip on some comfortable walking shoes, and embrace the cool evening air and go for a walk. It's a free and wholesome activity. Invite anyone who is available to join you.

If you are among those who make yearly resolutions to become more active or to get in shape, this can become one of the ways to do it. Going for a walk after dinner is also a good way to reflect upon the day. You can use this time to think about your work, or your finances, your relationships, and your faith. If you have someone with whom you can walk and converse, a post-dinner walk allows for venting of some of the day's frustrations. It gives you time to clear your mind. Later, when you get ready to turn in, your mind will be pleasantly clear of worries and concerns.

MINIMIZE YOUR WARDROBE

Most of us have more clothing than we realize. Yet, we wear only a small fraction of that clothing. A great way to begin a life beyond spending is to recognize the excesses in your life and begin to cut back, or pare down in these areas. I have noticed that I only wear a small percentage of the clothing that I own. It can be a very real eye-opener to look deep within the bowels of your closet and find clothing that you didn't even realize that you had, or, worse yet, that still has the store tags attached to them.

If you find yourself in this category, set aside a weekend and set aside room for two piles, one for the clothing you no longer want, and the other for the clothing that you want to keep. Perhaps the clothing that you normally wear is worn out, or perhaps you may be tired of those clothes. This may be a good time to give those clothes to the Goodwill or Salvation Army. Then, bring some of those un-worn, brand-new clothing from the back of the closet to the fore, and make those the 'new' clothes that you begin wearing, and put aside the brand-new clothing that you do not want, or can no longer wear, for the Goodwill or Salvation Army.

In my own life, I have found that I normally wear but a fraction of the total number of items in my wardrobe. However, the total size of my wardrobe has decreased considerably in the last few years. I believe that there are but a small number of experiences that are as wonderfully liberating as when I drop off a sizable donation to the Salvation Army. I then feel I am truly free as a bird, unburdened by a sizable wardrobe that I have to lug around with me like a dead albatross around my neck. By minimizing your wardrobe, you too can enjoy this feeling of emancipation from the dead weight of excess materialism.

GO TO BED EARLIER

As time goes by, I have found that I can no longer get by on the four-hour-a-night sleep schedule that I had while in college. I was in my early to mid-twenties, and so it was easy for me to make up for the short night by doubling up on my morning coffee and getting by, somehow, throughout the day. Now, fifteen years later, I find that this is no longer the case. It has become painfully clear to me that I can no longer maintain that regimen. This is why I now go to bed much earlier than before. I am in bed no later than ten o'clock at night. This allows me to get up (reasonably) refreshed and ready to face the day.

If you are well-past your frenetic college days, you may want to consider going to bed earlier. Trust me; your body will thank you. I find that I have much fewer ailments, such as colds, since I began going to bed earlier. But the effects are not just physical. I have also found that my state of mind is also much, much brighter when I am rested. I don't have as many temper tantrums, and I don't feel as sad or depressed about life as I used to in my four-hours-a-night days. I have come to believe, wholeheartedly, that countless individuals don't recognize the moments when their body is over-tired, and, when they begin getting temperamental, or depressed and weepy, they focus on the issue at hand, rather than look beyond the issue to determine whether their emotional reaction might not actually be caused by an overly tired body. Now that I aim for at least seven, and possibly eight, hours of sleep most nights of the week, I have found my emotional state of mind to reflect a greater amount of equanimity. You might also be able to achieve this by making it a habit of going to bed earlier.

I cannot emphasize enough the benefits of going to bed earlier. Your immune system will greatly benefit from the increased hours of sleep. Nothing can leave your body open and vulnerable to infection like lack of sleep. By not giving your body the amount of sleep that it needs, you are pushing it beyond its capacities, and it will break down, much like any other system that is made to exert itself beyond its limits. Most people are fastidious about keeping their vehicles in top shape by making sure that their cars have sufficient gasoline, oil, transmission fluid, and other essential items in their proper quantities. Yet, when it comes to sleep, most folks are only too happy to stay up past their bedtime and to rob their bodies of one of the most essential activities for sound health: sleep.

The need for sleep cannot be overestimated. It is well-known that lack of sleep has been used as a form of torture for prisoners of war. If it has been used as an instrument of torture, then why in the world would we want to torture ourselves by robbing ourselves of the divine sweetness of sound slumber? Do your body and your state of mind a favor. Give yourself a full night of sleep. I can almost guarantee you that you will awake feeling refreshed, relaxed, and having sufficient quantities of patience. The driver who cuts you off in the morning commute will no longer cause you as much rage. Your supervisor's nagging won't send you over the edge. The world will suddenly seem a little friendlier as a result of your restful night. Try it. You'll soon get hooked!

WAKE UP EARLIER

I witness a social phenomenon nearly every morning on the way to work. I get on the freeway, and, inevitably, I see people weaving in and out of lanes in their (seemingly) desperate attempt to get to wherever they need to go. Most likely, they are on their way to work. What confounds me is that these people most likely own an alarm clock. Most people that work rely on some sort of morning alarm to wake them up and remind them that they have to go to work. However, it clearly seems to escape their minds that they could set their alarms a half hour earlier, allowing them the opportunity to have at least half an hour more in their morning routine to get to work.

This way, they don't have to speed and weave their way in and out freeway lanes, as well as drive their heart rate and blood pressure up, every morning as they drive (past the speed limit) to work. Not only is this daily routine bad for their cardiovascular and immune systems, but it also runs the risk of getting a speeding ticket, which, these days, are quite expensive. An argument could be made that it is difficult enough to wake up at the ordinary time in the morning and how-could-I-possibly-get-up-any-earlier? But, the flaw in this line of reasoning is that it overlooks the fact that most people can (and possibly should) go to bed earlier, thus making it easier to wake up earlier, with the minimum of moaning and groaning.

This way, by going to bed earlier, and waking up earlier, a person can get (roughly) seven or eight hours of sleep, and wake up refreshed, and get ready to drive to work with more lead time, and therefore avoid the pressure of driving to work with only minutes to spare, or the uncomfortable feeling of getting to work late. Your immune system will be made stronger by the extra sleep, you'll be clear-headed, and have time to spare as you drive calmly and leisurely to work. Your boss will be impressed by how punctual you are, and you won't arrive at work frazzled by the stressful commute and angry at the drivers who didn't want to drive as fast as you did. If there are television shows that you want to watch but are broadcast late at night, simply program your entertainment system to record it for you, and this way to you can watch it the next day when you come home from work, rather than stay up late and suffer the consequences the next morning.

ENJOY POWER NAPS

This idea assumes that there is enough time in the day, but, a power nap can make a big difference in your energy level. If you get an hour for lunch at your job, use fifteen of those minutes for the actual consumption of your meal, and use the remaining forty five minutes to take an invigorating power nap. The risk of napping too long is that you may find yourself waking up not feeling refreshed at all. Instead, you may find that you are feeling sleepy the rest of the day. Thus, a forty five minute nap may be the ideal amount of time for you to feel refreshed and rejuvenated. Fewer minutes might not be enough time and more than that might cause you to feel too woozy to work.

Power naps are a great way to maintain your productivity. When most people think of napping, their image may be that of a lazy person who sleeps instead of works. And, although that might be true of some individuals, the smart ones use power naps to increase their productivity, rather than decrease it. A power nap is a great way to recharge the body, and it allows you to return to your work with a calm, but steady and focused mind. It's a way of ensuring a steady output of work, rather than to work until you drop.

Instead of working continuously from dawn to dusk, naps are a way to recover some of the energy lost during the morning, and putting it towards the productivity of the afternoon. This way, when you come home, you won't feel as bone-tired as you normally might. And, as a result, you'll have more energy for your loved ones, or pets, or hobbies when you come home from work. And, of course, everyone is different, so a forty five minute nap may be a little too long or too brief for your needs. Try napping at different intervals to see what the optimum period of time is for your body and mind.

TRY A NEW SPORT

I think that most people have had the experience of wondering what it would feel like to try a new sport. Perhaps we were changing channels on television and saw a sport being played by two professional national or international rival teams. Enjoying a sport is like enjoying a hobby, with some exercise being thrown into the mix. If you have never tried basketball, or golf, but have always wondered what it would be like to actually play the game, give it a try. There may be a city league in your home town, or there may be a few people in the office who get together on a regular basis to play a sport.

If you have a friend who plays golf on a regular basis, you may want to join that person and see what it feels like to swing correctly and hit a golf ball. Sports are a fun way to get in shape, and to make friends and meet interesting people. Perhaps you have played one sport for a long time and want to try a different one. Or, you may have spent most of your youth with your face buried in a book, and now want to expand your horizons and add a sport to the mix in order to have a more well-rounded life. And, in the end, you may find that the sport that you wanted to try was not as interesting or engaging as you thought. It's possible. But, as they say, you'll never know unless you try it.

By trying a new sport, you may find that you have a talent which you may not have, as yet, discovered. Also, by trying a new sport, you will get the opportunity to exercise a different set of muscles than the ones which you ordinarily exercise in your routine. Having a variety of sports keeps the process of exercising fresh and exciting. And, certain sports are seasonal. For example, skiing is a winter sport. Beach volleyball is enjoyed by many during the summer months. Therefore, the benefit of enjoying a variety of sports is that you can always look forward to being able to enjoy a sport, no matter what month or season of the year.

Also, by trying a new sport, you'll keep your mind sharp and attentive, and that is a great way to keep your mental abilities as bright and alert as always. Each sport has its rules, and therefore, by learning a new sport, you will have to become familiar with its rules, and this is the part that will keep your mind as sharp as a tack! Even if you don't end up embracing the new sport, your mind will benefit from the expansion you provided in learning the techniques and rules of the sport. At any rate, sports are a great way to get fresh air and to meet new and interesting people. You may end up meeting very nice people and gain a few friends in the bargain.

CATEGORY V

Your Social World

FIND A PEN PAL

Although the advent of social media sites such as MySpace, Facebook, and Twitter have all but rendered the idea of a pen pal rather passé, the idea of staying in touch with someone far away still holds an attraction to many people. I suppose it stems from the fact that we are, as they say, social creatures, or perhaps because no one wants to feel alone, or cut off from the world, but the idea of having a friend with whom you can correspond has always had great appeal to many people. It's fun to receive letters, either through the U.S. Mail, or in electronic form, from someone with whom we've developed an attachment. The idea of pen pals also had appeal for other reasons.

By having a pen pal from another country or from another culture, you get to learn how people live in other parts of the world. Perhaps you've stayed in touch with someone who lives in a country where the style of life is very different from what you're used to, or where the culture seems interesting or exotic, or all of the above. Having a pen (or keyboard) pal allows us to feel that we are not alone in this world, and that there are people who know we exist and who want to hear from us, and who want to share their corner of the world with us. The irony of the Internet is that it allows us to have so much more access to the world than ever before. At the click of a mouse you can go to the website of the University of Salamanca, or book a room in a hotel in Beijing.

And, yet, on some level, I think that there is a need for people to connect, and that need is just as strong as ever before, and I am not convinced that the Internet can fill that void. The appeal of a pen pal was that it allowed you to receive a hand-written letter from someone who took the time to actually use a pen and paper to express their thoughts in their own hand. By reading the letter that was hand-written, you were able to connect in a more personal way than through an e-mail, which shows nothing of a person's inner nature, other than through the tone of the words and the matter being discussed.

These days, there are online sites that 'match' you to a pen pal, so what exists right now is a synthesis between the old-fashioned pen pal system with the newer and instantaneous form of electronic communication inherent in social media sites. As with the other suggestions in this book, I highly recommend that you try having a pen pal in order to connect to people you might not normally connect to, and in the process enjoy the opportunity to learn about a different culture. And, who knows, if you ever travel to the part of the world where your pen pal resides, you may end up meeting your pen pal face-to-face, or you may end up being the tour guide if your pen pal takes a vacation and finds him or herself in your neck of the woods.

Reconnect with Friends

In our busy world, and with the hectic and frenetic pace of our daily lives, it is very easy to lose touch with people, even those with whom we have a strong attachment. If you find yourself in this category of people, set aside time each week to reach out to people with whom you wish to continue enjoying contact. And, if you have a bad (or filled up) memory, write it in your calendar to call or e-mail someone whose friendship means a lot to you. In our modern world, it's rather easy to let friendships slide. And, of course, this is not the result of willful neglect on our part. This is simply the end result, or byproduct, of the pace of modern living. Most of us come home tired, attend to our families and pets, cook and eat dinner, watch television and head off to bed. We wake up the next day and repeat the entire process all over again, five days a week, fifty weeks a year.

Therefore, the time and energy invested in the development and nurturance of friendships is something that can only be accomplished through conscious effort. It's very important to have friendships, as they allow us to feel connected to, and an integral part of, the intricate fabric of humanity. Friends allow us to feel loved and cared for, and they allow us to feel valued for who we are, without any sort of prejudice or ulterior motives. It can be a great source of comfort for us to have friends whose love and support can carry us through the most difficult and trying times in our lives. And, of course, the other great source of pleasure of having friends is the fact that we too can give of ourselves to them, and give them the love and support that they need when they encounter stormy seas in their lives.

Being able to reconnect with friends allows us to feel needed and important once again. The love and fellowship which friendship brings is priceless. If you have felt cut off or estranged from your friends, cultivating the reconnection with your friends will give you the opportunity to feel needed once again. Friendship is one of the most important and nourishing sources of love and connectedness that is available to us. Bask in its glow. Celebrate your friends, and allow them to celebrate you.

WORK ON YOUR RELATIONSHIPS

In our busy world, even those of us with the full awareness of the need to nurture relationships can fall prey to the rapid tempo of our daily lives and allow our relationships to become neglected. Relationships, of every type, are much like flowers or plants - they need continuous care, sunlight, and water, or else they whither. It's important to take time out of each day to express to those closest to us how much they mean to us, and how much we value them. It doesn't take a lot of effort to do this. But, it's an investment of time, and the dividends, in the form of healthy and vibrant relationships, are well worth it.

It is perhaps in these difficult and economically challenging times that it is even more important to express to those around us how much they mean to us, and how much we need them. In our country's past, it was the rugged individual who was able to make a name for him or herself, but, two hundred years after the days of the frontier, no one can really afford to live like that anymore. We all need each other, in an intricate web of human interdependency. Most of us cringe when we think of 'needing' other people, or else we entertain some far-flung vision in our minds of a neurotic and clingy person who demonstrates an excessive amount of need.

Neither the lonesome individual nor the needy neurotic are appropriate models of what we should strive for in our daily lives. We are connected to everyone else, and can maintain both a healthy independence as well as an appropriate level of interdependence on our fellow man. Once we can find this careful interplay, we can then find ways to keep our relationships healthy while at the same time honoring ourselves, and our own individual identities. As with so many areas of our lives, the scale has to be evenly weighed between independence and interdependence. Again, balance is the key.

NURTURE YOUR FRIENDSHIPS

Friendships are but another subcategory of relationships, and a very important one at that. Friendships are the buoys that can keep us afloat in stormy seas, and they are also the sails that allow us to capture the wind and soar through the ocean. Friendships are a treasure trove of shared memories, laughter, tears, and refuge when life becomes dark and it seems that life is conspiring against us. Friendships allow us to look beyond ourselves and to engage with other people whose backgrounds may be of stark contrast with that of our own. At the same time, friendships allow us to find other people whose vision, values and sensibilities might be mirror images of our own. Friendships are a safeguard and insurance against feeling too alone in the world. They allow us to enjoy simple companionship and camaraderie.

Yet, even the best of friendships can become strained now and again. If this happens to you, and the friendship is one which you wish to preserve, try to find a way to reach out and reconnect with that friend. Perhaps, if the source of declension was one of the "forbidden" topics of conversation, such as politics or religion, you may want to steer clear of that reference point, and stick to more neutral topics. And, sometimes, a simple apology is all it takes to reestablish a connection with a friend. At that point, if the other person is willing to accept said apology, the friendship can reestablish the closeness that had been enjoyed by both individuals.

Friendships are among some of the most important relationships that we can enjoy. Our society, as well as the entertainment industry, are constantly focusing only on romantic relationships as the source of passion and magic in our world. And, romantic relationships definitely have their place in our lives. Yet, romantic relationships are but one type among many different categories of relationships. Therefore, in addition to the other relationships in your life, nurture your friendships. Give them the love, water and sunshine that they deserve, and they will, indeed, blossom.

LOOK FOR GROUPS IN YOUR CITY

Although city life can certainly present its challenges, and its unsavory aspects, it also is able to offer us some unique opportunities. Most cities have clubs and social organizations which can become a great venue in which to socialize and make new friends. Look up the social clubs in your city, and, most likely, you'll come across a variety of social service organizations, such as, the Lions Club, Toastmasters International, and Kiwanis. You may want to check these clubs out. Call them and ask them what they do, and how often they meet. You may also want to inquire on the matter of how much they charge for membership.

By joining a social service organization, you'll be able to connect with others who also share your vision of service to the community. You never know what kind of friendships may develop as a result of being a member of these organizations. Having a shared sense of vision always provides the mortar that can help people bond, even over a very long period of time. I remember speaking to a gentleman some years ago, and he told me that he still stayed in touch with his fraternity brothers from the university which he attended. It is akin to the friendships that can develop between soldiers in the armed forces. You may also want to consider a city sports team. and get to know other adults who share your excitement for bowling, or hiking. There are Sierra Club chapters in many cities. Therefore, if being close to nature is one of your interests, you may want to consider joining a local chapter of the Sierra Club.

By looking for groups that you can join in our city, you can enjoy the feeling of being embedded and connected to your community. I believe that many of our citizens no longer feel connected to the communities in which they live. By finding groups that may share your interests or hobbies, you will have the opportunity to feel included and valued in your community. This will allow you to include and value others in your community, and thus allow you to forge new alliances and friendships. Civic, service, and support groups are a terrific way to reclaim the feeling of connectedness that has become eroded in many of our cities and communities.

RECONNECT WITH FAMILY

This is a rather sensitive topic as many families have their 'sensitive' areas in terms of family members not getting along, or the proverbial "bad seed" who never seems to get his or her act together and seems to drag down the entire family, like dead weight. Nevertheless, barring some of these more sensitive cases, you may want to examine the dynamics of your family and see if you can reconnect with members of your family with whom you've become estranged or simply lost touch. It can be a rewarding feeling to regain a sense of closeness that had been lost due to geographic distance, or the passage of time. Sometimes, all it takes is a telephone call, or a nice letter or e-mail.

Part of the reason why it may be difficult to reach out to family is that in our modern society, we are so busy and absorbed in the daily grind of working or going to school, buying groceries and paying the bills, that it becomes very easy to slip into a daily pattern of existence that does not incorporate other people into that pattern. And, in all fairness to everyone, it is really no one's fault. It is simply a sad statement of our existence, and our modern urban society. Nevertheless, you may find it a rewarding and enriching experience to reach out to family that you have not seen in a while.

In the end, blood is thicker than water. Thus, if you feel that you have become estranged from your own blood family, work up the strength to set things right with the relatives with whom you have held a grudge or with whom you have not spoken to in many years. Don't hold onto grudges. They have a way of eroding your heart and your health. If anything, allow yourself the opportunity to get things off your chest before it's too late. You may feel the relief of being able to communicate your feelings to a family member who hurt you. Even if he or she does not have the presence of mind to be able to understand and empathize with you, the experience of speaking your mind and reaching out to the other person may afford you the opportunity to reestablish the connection you may have felt that you had lost.

START A CLUB

Another way to meet people and make friends is to start a club. If the club you want does not exist, then you may want to try starting one of your own. There are so many hobbies and activities that lend themselves to a club, such as sewing, knitting, crocheting, photography, and hiking, just to name a few. You may want to place an ad on-line explaining that you are interested in starting a club based on a certain interest, and see what happens. You may be surprised! In starting a club of your own, you will not only be able to socialize, but you will also be able to practice and demonstrate some leadership skills.

I once started a local writer's group not far from my home a few years ago, and it was quite rewarding. Two members of our group became engaged, and so that only added to the vivacity of our club. Therefore, be open to what may come your way in such a setting. But the important thing is that you get to create new and meaningful friendships based upon a common interest. What may add to the success of the venture is creative and strategic advertising. If you're thinking of starting a hiking club, then you may want to go to local sport equipment stores, and ask them if they have a bulletin board. If they do, leave some fliers of your new club there. Or, if you would like to start a club based upon a religious tradition, then start by visiting some local churches or temples, and ask them if you can put fliers on their bulletin board.

Once you have a group up and running, you may want to consider appointing some of the members to key positions, or to give them key responsibilities. If the club is to run on dues, then appoint someone who is capable as the treasurer. Or, if the club meetings tend to run overtime, then you may want to consider appointing someone as the timekeeper. Another person could be placed in charge of the calendar, or the newsletter. Someone could be the recruiter, or the person in charge of advertising. The sky is the limit.

Take some time and write a list of your most honored hobbies, the ones you would enjoy even if you were stranded on a desert island. Timing may be key. In the wintertime, people may be more apt to stay indoors. During the summer months, people are more likely to be out and enjoying the outdoors, so also use the time of year as a guide in order to make informed decisions as to when and where to start a club. Obviously, it helps to live within driving distance of a mountain range if you are considering organizing a skiing club. Equally, it is necessary to be close to a coast if you want to start a surfing club. Give it some thought. You may decide not to do it. However, if you have always wanted to lead a group of your own, this may be the way to gain that experience.

JOIN A SOCIAL SERVICE CLUB

One of the most rewarding experiences in life is to feel that your actions are dedicated to, and in service of, our world. These experiences may come once in a while in your life, or you may one of the lucky ones who gets to experience this feeling rather frequently. One of the great things about a social service club is that you not only get a chance to meet new people, but you also get the opportunity to feel that what you are doing is of service to others. I once volunteered half a Saturday to serving at a food donation processing facility. All of us appeared early in the morning in jeans and t-shirts. We spent the next several hours sorting oranges, canned goods, and other perishable merchandise that was to be distributed to a local soup kitchen.

It was a great feeling to know that my hard work was being done to help poor or indigent families have a nutritious meal. It is a large processing plant and they pack the leftover produce and canned goods from nearby sources to be distributed to homeless and needy families. This packing facility is always welcoming volunteers. I was able to meet some very nice individuals who also shared my sense of volunteerism and a sense of service. Too often in our society, we get caught up in our wonderment of how a particular situation or relationship is going to benefit us. We want to know about, and be reassured of, the benefits that are coming our way as a result of our participation in a certain event, or our membership in a certain civic group.

Yet, life does not always evolve around our own benefit. Our own advantage is something our society wants us to be preoccupied about, but we don't have to behave that way. Our society wants us to be always caring about our own pleasure, or our own gain over others in a very competitive way. Yet, most of our religious traditions teach us that our primary mission on Earth is to be of service to our fellow man. There are numerous examples in the Bible and in Eastern religions which reinforce this view. We are not here to benefit solely for ourselves, and we are not here to benefit for ourselves at the expense of others.

Perhaps you may want to donate time to a local nursing home, or tutor students who are having difficulty with their classes. Believe it or not, there are many adults who are barely literate. You may want to find an organization that lets qualified volunteers spend time with adults who have difficulty reading and serving as their tutors. My local public library has a tutoring program that is very well run and organized. Use the Internet to find our which social service clubs exist in your city. You may be pleasantly surprised!

CATEGORY VI

Being of Service

Become a Big Brother or Big Sister

As I mentioned in the earlier section, one of the best ways to feel that you are making a difference in the world is by volunteering time to be of service to others. A wonderful way of doing this is to become a Big Brother or a Big Sister to a child who needs a mentor or role model. Being a Big Brother or Sister provides you the privilege of becoming a source of inspiration to a child who may not otherwise have any prosocial role models. One of the saddest statements of our society is that we do not have enough role models for young people to emulate and from whom they can learn. As a result, they turn to rap singers, and other adults from dubious backgrounds to choose as their role models.

As a Big Brother or Big Sister, you have the opportunity to be a wholesome role model to a young person who needs mentoring. As a Big Brother or Sister, you can take the child out to museums and other educational places that may not otherwise be available to that young person. Many modern students are not exposed to classical music, and so a trip to listen to a local symphony may be a very meaningful treat to an underprivileged student. You may also want to be a tutor for that student and to be of help with their schoolwork or their homework. Many students fall very far behind in their schoolwork because they are too timid to ask for assistance with their studies. As a Big Brother or Sister, you can break through that wall of silence and find out if a student has need for additional assistance in a school subject.

In the end, perhaps nothing is nearly as noble as the act of passing on accumulated knowledge and wisdom to an eager and open-minded student. Being a Big Brother or Big Sister will allow you the privilege of being able to pass down the wisdom which you have (hopefully) accumulated over the years. By passing knowledge and wisdom down to an eager understudy, you will allow your Little Brother or Little Sister the chance to learn from your mistakes. This may allow him or her to have a smoother sail through the ocean of life. After all, if they avoid your mistakes, and only make their own, your mission is fulfilled.

MENTOR SOMEONE

When I am asked why we are here on Earth, my immediate answer to the query is simple: We are here to serve others. At least, that is my own personal belief. This view is informed by my own Judeo-Christian upbringing. I still hold to the view that we are here to serve others. One great way to serve another human being is to serve as a mentor. I believe that one of the most unfortunate aspects of our society is that young people do not have enough role models to emulate. What is badly needed is a National Mentoring Program, one in which each state would have its own chapters, and people could be screened and matched to the appropriate student.

Young people need more guidance and mentoring than is provided by our society. Consider the fact that more and more families have both parents working outside the home just to make ends meet. If they are doing this just so that they can afford time at a local ski lodge, then that's a different matter altogether. But for the parents who are both working in order to pay the bills and send their children to schools, there may be some untoward negative effects as a result. It is no mystery that many children in such homes lack supervision and guidance. These are the young people who end up experimenting with drugs, alcohol, and sex. This is why a national mentoring program may be the way to get these "latchkey children" out of those unsupervised environments and into a closely structured environment where they can continue to work on their studies and learn other recreational activities, such as sports or a musical instrument.

Nevertheless, until such time as these centers are founded or established (if they ever are), then it falls on ordinary citizens like us to serve as mentors to students who need additional guidance or tutoring. Mentoring can be a great way to demonstrate prosocial behaviors, and to serve as a rich source of wisdom and intellectual furtherance. You may want to look online for local mentoring programs where you live. Being able to provide a young person with supplemental guidance and placing them on the right track can be a greatly rewarding experience, reinforcing the age-old adage that it is more rewarding to give than to receive.

VOLUNTEER AT A HOMELESS SHELTER

In our consumerist society, it is so easy to fall into the trap of thinking about the next item that we want to purchase, or the next big vacation that we want to finance. Yet, we must not forget that there are others who are not as fortunate as ourselves. I regularly see homeless persons as drive to and fro in the communities close to where I live. One of my friends recently remarked that he is seeing more and more homeless persons and they are not the 'traditional' ethnic persons that we are used to seeing on the streets. Rather, he stated, these are White Anglo-Saxon Protestants who seemed to have been recently displaced.

Therefore, we can no longer make snide remarks about 'certain groups' in our society who lack the industriousness to pull themselves up by their bootstraps. Almost, everyone, it seems, has been affected by the downturn in the economy in the last several years. By volunteering time at a homeless shelter, one is brought into direct contact with those who have become the dispossessed and the disenfranchised. They are not any different from you and me. These individuals have the same human needs as we do. They need work, food, clothes, and love. It is true that many veterans and many persons with severe mental illness make up definitive sub-populations of the entire homeless population. And yet, even those individuals are also human beings who deserve to be treated with dignity and respect.

By donating time at a homeless shelter, and by seeing that so many of these individuals do not have even the basics that we take for granted, we can begin to realize just how much "stuff" we feel that we cannot live without. And yet, these are things that are entirely superfluous. The worst part of it is that our capitalistic society wants to convince us that we truly "need" a bigger television, a faster computer, a new car, or a phone with more apps on it. And, we fall for it. We fall for the advertising. We fall for the splashy ads, and the fancy packaging. There is one brand of rum that is sold in a beveled glass decanter, and the label is printed on what appears to be parchment. It looks like it was brought right up from an old pirate shipwreck. It looks so nice that one is tempted to just buy it and use for decoration, but never to consume it. I tried that, but nevertheless fell victim to the temptation to imbibe it.

My point is that advertisers are keen in using packaging and advertising that convinces us that we "must" get the latest product that they are selling. You can even here it in the radio ads: "Hurry now to your local ---- dealer!" Yes, hurry! Run! However, these days, I make it a point to run but in the opposite direction. I run away from that kind of pressure. However, if you work with homeless people, you can see how we have all been duped by corporate America into believing that acquiring goods will be part of the American Dream. Yes, it is corporate America that is 'dreaming' that we'll fall for their little spending traps. Trust me, you'll return home and feel positively guilty about even a modest amount of goods.

VOLUNTEER AT A CONVALESCENT HOME

Convalescent homes are sometimes transitional places where patients need more care than they can receive at home but are no longer so ill that they need to remain in the hospital. These are places where some people volunteer to spend time with the patients so that they do not feel abandoned or lonely. This may represent yet another venue where you may to consider volunteering some of your spare time. Think of the happiness that your presence (assuming that you have a presence that brings happiness) will bring to a patient who otherwise has no one to talk to in these facilities. Many times, the nurses are busy doing their rounds and they may not have the time necessary to spend much time socializing with their charges.

With state budgets being constricted, these are the times during which facilities such as nursing homes will benefit from the dedicated efforts of a volunteering staff who can supplement the services of the paid staff. One can also gain a richness of experience by volunteering time with the patients in a convalescent home. They have lived interesting lives and have gained a certain amount of wisdom which some of them (perhaps not all) might be willing to share with someone who is willing to listen to them. Older persons have a world of learning inside of them. It is so very unfortunate that in our society, it is young people who are the driving force in the marketing of products, goods, and services. Movies, music, and television are all dominated by the 12 to 18 year old consumer crowd. Yet, in more traditional Asian countries, it is the elders who are sought and consulted because of their learning and their wisdom.

By volunteering time at a convalescent home, you can come into direct contact with the wisdom and the wealth of knowledge that the patients have accumulated. All they want, besides recovering from their illnesses, is someone with whom they can converse and not feel lonely. By volunteering a few hours a week in a convalescent home, you will feel the rewarding feeling that comes from a sense of service, and from knowing that you helped touch the life of an individual who benefited from your company. Just being able to help someone smile is gift enough. Holding someone's hand can also be a wonderful way to help a patient feel cared for and loved. So many studies have demonstrated strong evidence that the healing power of touch is more powerful than had been previously known or acknowledged. Babies who are not held enough after birth fail to thrive. Why should it not be as necessary for an elderly person to be touched gently as well?

TEACH SOMEONE TO READ

In our educationally advanced society, it is easy to forget that there are those who cannot read or write. A wonderful way to volunteer time every week, or whenever free time becomes available, is to help teach someone how to read and write. This problem is likely to become worse due to the overwhelming number of immigrants who come to the United States lacking even basic grammatical knowledge of the English language. Many of these immigrants had to begin working while they were very young and were not given the chance, indeed the privilege, of attending school. And, upon arrival in the United States, their first priority is to find any sort of employment, no matter how menial, so that they can support their families. Thus, their whole lives are spent laboring for minimum wages and they are never given the chance to further their education.

By giving up some of your free time to help an illiterate adult or student how to read or write, you will be opening up an entire new world for them. The things that you and I take for granted, like the dozens of books that we can buy or check out of library, and even the fact that you are able to read, at this very moment, the words that I have typed on this page, are all derivative of the fact that we are literate adults. The other activities that have become commonplace, such reading e-mails, and sending texts, are also stemming from the fact that we are literate. Yet, for many of these adults, immigrant and even many native-born Americans, these activities are shrouded in mystery.

Teaching someone to read and write requires an inordinate amount of patience and understanding. Therefore, if you are considering serving others as a literacy tutor, remember that your patience will be tested, time and again. What children learn quickly, adults may take twice the amount of time to learn. Therefore, consider this activity carefully before you jump into it. Also, remember that adults who are illiterate require a structured approach to learning. It is not enough to simply crack open the local newspaper and expect them to start learning how to read in a few short sessions. Yet, think of how wonderful it could feel if you were to help an adult learn how to read and write. What a gift that would be!

TUTOR A STUDENT

Students need more guidance and nurturing than most people realize. What makes this task so difficult is that so many students need the tools that ought to be provided at home, but they are not given these tools. Instead, many students live in homes where both parents work, and therefore receive the minimum of educational guidance or assistance. Other students come from broken homes, and are being raised by a single parent, usually the mother. Therefore, the academic instruction which they receive in the classroom will be all they have to guide their intellectual development.

Yet, remember that many of our public school classrooms are populated with up to thirty five students, and sometimes even more. Therefore, the overburdened teachers are not able to spend much time with each and every student, consequently, it should be a surprise to no one that so many of these students begin to sink and slide backwards, and eventually drop out. So, by volunteering time to tutoring a student, you will be making an invaluable contribution to the educational future of the students of the United States.

Our country truly needs more volunteers who can supplement the efforts being made by teachers and educators. There is only so much that they can do. The issue becomes much more complicated by the fact that some people feel that it is the ineffective teachers who are only adding to the problem. Yet, it is not within the scope of this book to address the issue of tenure and the inherent difficulty in replacing incompetent educators. Suffice it to say, it will be of extraordinary benefit to our society to have an army of volunteers who can spend time each week with students who need supplemental instruction.

Some students may have learning disabilities that go undetected and undiagnosed. Others may simply be a little slower than their peers. Yet, regardless of the reason, it is imperative that something be done to improve the educational outcomes of countless students. Volunteering time each week with a student contributes toward the kind of investment our nation must make in education. Our government spends billions of dollars on questionable wars and then makes cuts in the amount of money invested toward education.

This is where I believe our national policies and priorities are not what they should be. They are short-sided and are not the kind of long-term growth investment decisions that need to be made. In order for our Republic to not only survive but thrive in the twenty first century, our leaders need to allocate more resources for education. That is what will create the bright, visionary and contributing future citizens that we all hope will populate our country in the years to come. Volunteering time with a student may seem like a drop in the Education Bucket, but it is these tiny drops in a bucket that build up over time. You might even look back to a time in your own life when you benefited from some supplemental instruction, and how comforting it was to know that someone was going to help you understand concepts which before were difficult to grasp.

DONATE BLOOD

One of the most profoundly personal things that one human being can do for another is to offer the very source of our life and energy -- our blood. Giving blood is not just a task or routine. You are giving up the very substance on which our lives depend. Giving blood represents the ultimate in selflessness. You are literally spilling your blood to help another human being who may need it. We early get the opportunity to see or get to know the persons who benefit from our biological donations. Yet, imagine how profoundly moving and deeply touching it would be to get to know the person whose life we saved as a result of our blood donation. Imagine meeting them for the first time and realizing that they might not be alive were it not for our selfless efforts. Imagine hearing the voice of that person telling you that she might not be alive were it not for your blood. My partner gives blood on a yearly basis, and I know for a fact that she greatly values the sense of contribution that comes with it.

I would gladly donate blood myself were it not for the fact that I tested positive for tuberculosis in 1999. It never became a full-blown case, but, I was exposed to it, and so my body created antibodies against it. To this day, I can only get a chest x-ray whenever I get a new job or am otherwise required to get tested for tuberculosis. If you have never given blood before, remember that you may feel a little woozy afterward, and that your immune system will be lowered as a result of giving blood. But, with some rest and healthful food afterward, you should be just fine. I suppose that for many people, particularly those from the Midwest, there is a practicality to the whole thing: our bodies produce blood all the time, and, therefore, why not donate some in case some person may need it after an accident, etc.

For someone of a spiritual nature, however, the act of giving blood represents our sharing of the most profound energy in the universe with another person. God is in those red blood cells that we are donating. Remember, those cells are *alive*. They dance to the same rhythm of the universe as do the comets and the stars. Blood does not merely represent life. Blood is life, so much so that it has become almost mythologized. Most vampire stories revolve around the drinking of blood and the immortality that one can gain as a result. Jesus promised that anyone who would drink his blood would gain everlasting life. Therefore, blood has always been seen as the very source of life, and that life can be either mortal or immortal.

CATEGORY VII

Enjoying Nature

GO TO A LAKE

Lakes have a power all their own. They have a profoundly calming effect. When I was ten years old, I visited my aunt and uncle at their lake house outside Minneapolis. It seemed like a dream world. The combination of the lake and the dock that extended out onto the lake, as well as all the trees, made it a particularly cozy home, at least to my ten year old eyes. My aunt would complain about the cold Minnesota winters, but, since I visited their home in the summer, it seemed like Heaven to me. If you have the chance to visit a lake, by all means do so. Lakes generally are very calm, and they therefore possess a spiritual quality all their own.

The state of mind that one is able to achieve at a lake is a little different from the effect that a trip to the ocean can have. Lakes can be just as calming as the ocean, but in a very different way. It is as if the effect of being on a lake is immediately felt and recognized. There is an instant stilling of the mind and a tranquilizing of the soul. The effect of the ocean is different and no less special, but it is different nevertheless. Lakes are a perfect place to get away from it all, and to forget the trials and tribulations of ordinary city or urban life.

Going out onto the lake can be a wonderful way to feel the true stillness that a lake can offer. Lakes don't have the roiling waves and crashing sound that an ocean has. Lakes are gentle, and quiet. They seem to belong to a world all their own. If you can, try to visit a lake and experience the incredible stillness that a lake can offer. Lakes can offer us a glimpse into our own souls. They offer a chance at quiet contemplation. In a world as busy and as loud as ours, that can be a real blessing.

Lakes have beauty that is all their own. They provide the stillness where you can navigate the deepest depths of your own heart. Someone very wise once told me that the mind is much like the surface of a lake. The more calm and tranquil the waters, the deeper you can peer. Thus, lakes provide a living metaphor. They are places where we can find choppy, rough waters that allow us to view only superficial reflections. We cannot peer deeply. But, they are also a place where we can find the calmest waters imaginable. And, just like the still waters of a lake, your ability to search your own soul is based upon how calm and still your own mind is at the moment in which your peer into the depths. Calm the waters of your mind, and travel down into the depths of your heart and peer into the complex, mystical world of your own heart.

GO TO THE WATER'S EDGE

Having grown up in Long Beach, California, one of the great gifts of living in that city was its proximity to the ocean. For as far back as I can remember, the ocean has always been an integral part of my life. Whether it was as a curious toddler, or an awkward teenager, or a free-spirited college student, the ocean was my perpetual background. It was always there. To this day, whenever I go to the beach, my first thought is: "Why am I not here every day?" The ocean has a profoundly relaxing effect on me. The scale and scope of all my problems seem to reduce in size almost immediately. There is something magical about seeing the water from the distance, and being able to hear the waves, with their constant rolling sound, like thunder muted in water. Going to the beach is like going on vacation, even though I don't live that far from it.

Some people complain about the sand, and how it gets into every bodily cavity that it can find. However, I find that to be a small price to pay for the incredible gift of being able to see the place from which we crawled out eons ago. People can give rational reasons why they like to go to the beach. It's relaxing. It's a chance to get away from the city. It's a place where you can work on your tan, or read a book, without ever being bothered by anyone else. Yet, even with all of our rational reasons why we like to go to the beach, I believe that there is something underneath all of the rationalizations.

I believe that there is something more profound than all of the conscious reasons that people give as the reasons which purportedly explain why they go to the beach. I truly believe that the real reason that people go to the ocean is that we came from the oceans. We evolved from the water. It is a perfectly comfortable proposition for me that God created all living things, and that the evolution which took place on Earth was happening as a result of God's creative power. There is nothing incompatible between the beliefs that God created all life (Creationism), on the one hand, with the belief, on the other hand, that life evolved through natural selection into its permutations (Evolution).

Even with all of our sophistication, and our sense of knowing all that is knowable in our universe, I believe that it is our relationship with water, particularly the ocean, which has humans returning to it every summer. Let's face it, no one tells people to return to the water. No one tells them to go frolic in the waves. It's based upon our instinctual past. We came from the water. Our bodies are 70% water, and it reflects the fact that 70% of the Earth's surface is also made of water. Thus, even our bodies are a reflection of our watery heritage. Without water, complex life as we know it cannot exist.

LISTEN TO NATURE

One of the cassettes that I have enjoyed listening to the most over the years has been one which has the sounds of nature. We actually have a few of those in our home. Some have contained the sounds of a gentle brook rolling through a forest. Others have had the sounds of large waves crashing onto a beach. Yet others have had more 'exotic' sounds, like that of a lion roaring in the distance, or the sounds of wild parrots and howler monkeys in the rain forest. These cassettes were able to transport me to distant lands and to exotic destinations. However, their true value lay in their ability to keep me in touch with nature.

In the daily urban existence which I must maintain, I am regularly aware that as urban dwellers, urbanites are cut off from nature, with all of its blessings. The sounds of nature allow us to maintain a link to this world. It is not necessary to purchase a tape or CD with the sounds of nature, although it is a purchase which I do recommend. Consider it more of an investment than anything else. Yet, even without recorded sounds, one can keep a sharp ear out for the sounds of nature. One any day, even in some parts of a city, one can hear the fanciful chirping of birds. Some birds are quite elaborate with their little symphonies which they sing at the top of their little lungs. One can also hear dogs barking, as well as the gentle swaying of the trees during a windy day. Other sounds are quite impressive, such as the sound of thunder during a summer rain.

I believe that with the changing weather patterns, and with the need to procure employment, many people are now feeling somewhat trapped in their urban living spaces. This may explain why these tapes and CDs with the sounds of nature have become so popular. It reminds one of the computer screen savers which depict scenes of nature. People do whatever they can to carve out a niche of the natural world for themselves. If we can't reach nature, either because of where we live, or our time and resources limit the amount of time that we can live next to nature, then we will bring nature to our CD players or our computer screens. But, even if it is on an occasional basis, it is a very replenishing activity to turn an attentive ear to the natural world and to allow its natural sounds to soothe our minds, and assuage our souls.

TAKE A WALK IN A PARK

Parks represent a slice of the natural world in the middle of a city. Parks have been a setting for families to have picnics and have relaxed gatherings for years. Parks can still be a nice way to enjoy a little piece of nature in the middle of a city. They can be a pleasant way to enjoy a mid-day meal. I have seen so many places of employment in cities where, at twelve noon, countless employees from various corporate entities file out of their offices, dressed in their weekday best, and head out to the local eateries to 'socialize.'

Young people in their twenties in particular, seem more prone to do this. I don't know if it's because they are taken in by the jet set office environment, and because they want to feel important that they are willing to go out to expensive restaurants and pay a lot of money in order to feel like high-rollers. But, these are usually young people who are not even out of college, and are still racked with student loan debt, and a host of other bills to pay. Yet, rather than learn to become thrifty, they file out of the offices where they work, and head to the nearest upper-end eatery, and pretend to be something they're not -- wealthy. I don't know if it's human nature to want to feel important, that we matter. Or, perhaps what I witness is purely the vanity of youth.

Nevertheless, these are the spending patterns that become engrained, and unless something is done to correct these habits, they can lead straight to bankruptcy. What a lot of young people forget to do is to annualize their expenditures. If they spend an average of ten dollars a day (which is quite conservative) on lunch, that comes out to fifty dollars in a week, or two hundred dollars a month. But, on an annual basis, that comes out to $2400 in a single year, just on lunch. That's not counting the amount spent on meals out on the weekends. It certainly adds up!

What makes these habits hard to break is that there may be psychological reasons behind the behavior. Perhaps young people go to these restaurants *en masse* because they cannot stand the thought of sitting under a tree with a brown bag lunch and eating alone. Perhaps it goes further back to our childhood days when some of us may have felt left out and sat alone and watched everyone else go out and play. For a lot of people, being part of the in-crowd is very important, so important in fact that they are willing to sacrifice part of their yearly salary (because that is what it boils down to) in order to be part of the in-crowd. In the end, it's a lifestyle choice. Some people are perfectly content sitting under a tree and enjoying a brown bag lunch which they brought from home. I am one of those people.

WATCH A SUNSET

Although the people who reside in the Polar Regions get to enjoy the Northern Lights, most of us get to enjoy a nice sunset every evening. Nature gives us a free light show every day, and so many of us simply ignore it. Yet, sunsets can be so beautiful to watch. Having grown up in Southern California, I have been blessed with the spectacle of sunsets over the Pacific Ocean, and they are truly a sight to behold. There is something so majestic and so grand about sunsets, and yet they are also so peaceful and tranquilizing. If you can, you may want to incorporate watching the sun set into your daily routine. Try to do it as often as you can spare the time for it. Don't take anything with you. Don't take your cell phone, or your iPad, or laptop computer. Just pull up a chair and allow the warmth of the sun to illuminate your skin.

So many of us are so plugged into our portable electronic gadgetry that we forget how nice it is to simply sit and enjoy something as beautiful as a sunset. I have seen so many young people at the beach who seem unable to put their iPhone or iPads down, or to put them away. Their behavior takes on a compulsive overtone, as if they will implode if they cannot be constantly plugged into their device. A social critic once wrote that it is like watching an infant who won't let go of its security blanket. Only now, we are watching adults who can't let go of their "security device." It is truly infantile and unsettling to be sure. Nevertheless, sunsets are a great opportunity to set aside all electronic gadgetry and to enjoy God's creation and to watch the sky and clouds turn all sorts of shades of pink and red. The best part of it is the fact that it does not cost you a penny to enjoy the spectacle. All you need is a comfortable chair and a willingness to clear your mind and to open your heart to the wonders of Mother Nature.

Sunsets signify the end of a day. Sunsets allow us to anticipate the setting of the sun on our own lives, so to speak. While watching a sunset, we can think about the end of our lives on Earth. Did we do all that we could do with the life and time that God gave us? Did we use our God-given talents as best as we could? Did we serve our fellow man as we should have? Sunsets are a good way to gauge whether we will get to the end of our lives with either joy in our hearts or whether we are headed towards an end filled with regret. Do not allow the end of our own life to be one of regret. The next time you watch a sunset, think about your own life. Then go do what you feel that you must do in order to feel that you have accomplished all of your goals. Make the sunset of your life a glorious and dazzling display of color and magic!

WATCH A SUNRISE

Most of us, me included, are too caught up in the rat race of modern life. We wake up, drag ourselves to the bathroom, shower, get dressed, eat breakfast, and drive off to work. Yet, due to the hectic and harried lifestyles that we live, there is another one of nature's miracles that we miss -- sunrises. Sunrises are very different from sunsets. A sunrise represents the promise of a new day. It is a symbol of a fresh start. A chance to begin again. Sunrises bring with them a sense of optimism, and the hope that today will be a better day than yesterday. Sunrises bring with them their own 'coziness', particularly with certain rituals, such as a nice warm shower, or the sight of a pot of rich-smelling coffee, brewing and percolating. Images of Continental breakfasts come to mind, with scrambled eggs, fresh fruit, cheese, and muffins, and other delectable goodies. One slips into fresh, clean clothing, laundered and pressed, ready for action.

There is a sense of hope that the day will fulfill all of the hopes and expectations that we have placed upon it. There is a charging up, rather than a letting down, as with sunsets. At any rate, if you have the chance, give yourself the opportunity to enjoy a sunrise, even if it's only on the weekend. Watching the sun rise is an amazing experience, and it is something that you can share with loved ones, or by yourself. As with the enjoyment of sunsets, try and enjoy the sunrise with no other sounds but the sounds of nature. While I lived briefly in Moldova, I would wake up every morning to the sound of a rooster crowing. It only added to the feeling of rustic simplicity in that part of Europe. You may want to savor the sunrise with some equally savory coffee and a blanket. These are little rituals which give life its meaning and its substance. They don't involve any outlays of money, and they connect us to nature, and to the rhythms of the universe.

Sunrises allow us to feel a sense of promise. They give us the anticipation that life will be better today than it was yesterday. Each new day brings with it the potential that life will become brighter, and that we are headed towards a future that is rosier than our past. The next time you watch a sunrise, offer up a little prayer asking God to make the day brighter than the day that preceded it. Life is a journey in which each day should bring more light and happiness than the day which came before it. Sunrises, therefore, represent the gift of eternal optimism and hope that life will get better. Think of each new day as a clean slate; a chance to start over and make your life the journey of bliss and magic that it was meant to be!

GO CAMPING

Camping is a great way to be surrounded and immersed in nature. Then, at the conclusion of the camping trip, you can then return home to urban life. In 1999, I went camping with a friend of mine. We took the train up to Merced, and from there took a bus to Yosemite. It was a great trip. I was fresh out of college, but still used to traveling like a poor student. We stayed in a camp where the tents were already set up with tougher-than-nails canvas. There was no work involved in setting up our base camp. It was like a little teepee village, and all of the other tents were also set up in the same fashion. We went hiking, took photos, and took a tour of the countryside.

Camping is a fun way to 'rough it up' and to leave the niceties of urban life behind and to focus on nature at its finest. There is nothing like the scent of pine trees and the sounds of different birds singing as you wind your way through a forest trail that looks pristine and timeless. I suppose that it is the timelessness of nature which may cause it to have such widespread appeal to so many people. In a forest, there is no such thing as 'outdated' or 'obsolete.' Nature reflects time in its rhythms and cycles, but at the same time, there is a suspension of time as well. It is paradoxical, and yet, that is where the appeal lies.

In nature we can see how life begins, flourished, reproduces, withers, and then dies. But, it is reborn again. Thus, the cycle is constantly regenerating itself. But, by being in nature, we are able to get away from wristwatches, calendars, alarms, and weekly and monthly planners. Nature allows us to be part of the rhythms of time but without the constant awareness of time such as our society demands of us. Camping allows us to reconnect to this natural world. If you live within driving distance of camping sites, give a weekend over to camping in the woods. You may very well find yourself coming back to the 'real world' rejuvenated and renewed.

Category VIII

Arts and Crafts

START A ROCK COLLECTION

Rocks are amazing natural objects. They tell their own stories. Some have come about as a result of incredible geologic processes. Others came about as a result of dramatic volcanic activity. Others have experienced the soothing, and smoothing, effects of a tranquil life lived on a riverbed. Others have been exposed to harsh desert environments, and bear the darkened crusts which attest to that effect. Whatever type of rocks you may find interesting, collecting rocks can be a great way of connecting to nature as well as a good educational tool. Some people even build themselves a "rock garden."

Rocks can be companions, and some have even used the well-known expression of referring to their stones as their 'pet' rocks. There are some stones whose appearance is beautiful, such as hematite, with its polished, silvery surface. Other forms of hardened minerals, such as crystals, also present some of the most beauteous forms to be found in nature. Quartz crystals, particularly in cluster form, are some of the most fascinating natural formations to be found in nature. Their attractiveness and their intrigue are wonderful. Of course, many people have ascribed healing properties to many types of stones and crystals. For example, many people believe that quartz has healing properties. Some believers wear amulets around their necks with a quartz crystal fastened to it. With their mysterious shapes and cool, crystalline form, it is no wonder that people are enchanted by these amazing natural gems.

Even if you don't personally believe in the magical properties of stones or crystals, they can become a part of your life as an interesting hobby. If you live near a river, or river bed, you can often find very beautiful stones absolutely free. It can be a fun family activity. You can even set up rock 'beauty contests' and award a prize to the owner of the rock deemed to be the most interesting, or visually appealing. Rocks can even be a way of studying other cultures. For example, the Japanese have their rock gardens, and the wavy lines that are created by a small rake in the gravel represent the waves of the ocean. Other cultures have used stones for ceremonial purposes. Even a trip to your local public library to check out books on rocks and gems can be an entertaining and educational way to spend a Saturday afternoon.

Of course, not all stones originate on Earth. Meteorites are stones that crash on our planet. Most come from the Asteroid Belt, in the region between the orbits of Mars and Jupiter. They also have very fascinating stories to tell us. This is another subject which I recommend reading about in a library book or on the internet. Collecting meteorites can be a very expensive hobby, thus, for the purposes of this book, which advocates a thrifty lifestyle, I recommend reading about them instead.

START A SEASHELL COLLECTION

This suggestion is obviously more practical if you live near the ocean, but, even if you don't, you can still enjoy this activity. Shells represent a link between the natural world and the critters that inhabit that world. Shells are the temporary shelter for crustaceans. They provide both an abode, as well as protection from the elements. And yet, for all of their 'practical' usage, shells have some of the most beautiful forms to be found in all of nature. The spiral shapes that define shells have a somewhat mesmerizing appeal. They are also incredibly strong, thus, shells represent a unique blend of esthetics and strength.

Starting a shell collection can be a great way to learn about life in the oceans. A casual stroll on the beach can be a great way to begin your collection. I have spent many an afternoon wading in the water, and have stumbled upon (literally) many wonderful shells, many of which are in my collection. Most of them are not very big, but they are very cute and worth keeping. Of course, no one described these marvels of nature more poetically than Anne Morrow Lindbergh, and I highly recommend reading her classic book, *A Gift from the Sea*, which she wrote while on retreat by the ocean.

The way I see it, shells connect us to the ocean. I have always wanted to feel, and do feel, connected to the ocean. It is a combination of factors which causes me to want this connection. First of all, it is spiritual, and I definitely feel closer to God at water's edge than I do even at some places of public worship. For me, the ocean is a place of public worship. I have prayed near the water, and felt connected to all of nature there. Secondly, it is said that all life began in our oceans. So, perhaps it is an ancestral tug that keeps bringing me back to the water. Our first nine months of life start in a watery enclosure, and seventy percent of our bodies are composed of water, which, interestingly, corresponds to roughly the same percentage of the Earth's surface being covered by water. Therefore, in a very real sense, we are watery beings. And, therefore, while holding a sea shell in my hand, I am reminded of our watery heritage.

START A LEAF COLLECTION

Leafs are the signature creations of the trees and plants that bore them. Leafs have always had a visual appeal to the countless people who behold them. Every year, many Americans flock to New England to see the leaves bear the colors of the autumn foliage. Even just by looking at photos of the New England forests, one is struck by the richness of the colors. A wild tapestry of yellow, brown, and orange colors on the ground. Leaves are like the pages of a book, each with its own narrative of the life of its parent tree or plant, just waiting to be told. Within each leaf, we see the stage of all of life: birth, growth, vibrancy, withering, and, finally, death.

Many people save leaves inside of a book, as a way of preserving their relationship to the leaf, and as a way of preserving the leaf itself. A leaf may represent a moment in time, or perhaps it may have been picked up during a particularly wonderful vacation. Or, a leaf may have been found during a stressful time in your life, and you picked it up for inspiration or as a sign of hope. Whatever the reason, a leaf is a nice small token of nature, and it can be stowed away without taking up much space. You may want to start collecting leaves throughout different parts of the year. Or, you could start a collection and gather leaves from as many different species of trees as you can find. This is also an educational activity and is one that can be shared with your young ones. They can be taught about the different types of trees that exist, as well as the way that plants and trees generate oxygen through the process of photosynthesis.

Leaves connect us to the vibrant patters that exist in nature. It is akin to the patterns that one can find in snowflakes. Each snowflake has its own unique shape and symmetry. Likewise, each leaf carries its own perfection. Hold one in your hand and marvel at the symmetry as well as the randomness of its design. In the end, we are like the leaves on a tree; each one of us carries our own unique patters, lines, colors and symmetries. That is what makes each one of us special in our own right.

TRY FINGER PAINTING

Finger paints are a highly entertaining way to enter the world of artistic creations. Art has been one of man's earliest recreational activities. But, art also became a way for man to record his early life, like the cave drawings in North American and in Europe, or the more elaborate forms as was later seen in Ancient Egypt and the Americas. Finger paint is an activity that can be enjoyed with the minimum of outlay. All you need are some primary colors, and some good quality paper or cardboard on which to paint, and that's it! Of course, you'll want to cover your floor with some garbage bags so as not to stain your linoleum or carpets.

Finger paints bring out the artist in everyone. In a sense, finger paints allow everyone to connect to their creative side. Too often, in our computerized world, we have become so used to pushing a button, or sliding our fingertip across a computer screen, that we have lost touch with the creative side of our brains. This is one of the unfortunate parts of our having to grow up and becoming responsible adults -- we lose touch with that creative spark that defined our younger years. And, this is also what I see happening to younger generations these days. They are being introduced to toy versions of laptop computers and play versions of cell phones.

The older games that I remember as a small child that involved real creativity, such as Legos, and Lights Alive, no longer seem popular these days. And, I believe that corporate entities are behind this. They are creating the toy versions of the cell phones and laptops so that when these youngsters grow up, they will already be 'primed' to buy these items. Get them started young. This way, they will be hooked into buying the real thing a few years down the road. Nevertheless, finger paints can be a great way to avoid this way of thinking. It's a way of getting back to basics - paint, cardboard, and your fingers. It doesn't get any more basic than that. And, the wonderful thing about basic art activities, is that they are low-cost, and can modified without incurring too much of an increase in cost. For example, if you tire of using your fingers, you can 'graduate' to using a small brush. Hobby paint brushes are still very inexpensive.

TRY PHOTOGRAPHY

Photography has not lost its artistic appeal. A well-taken photo is able to capture the wonder of a moment in time, and it is able to do this permanently. Photography, like painting, is an art form that almost anyone can try. There is no need to be another Ansel Adams. The important thing is that you allow yourself the freedom to try a new creative medium through which you can express yourself. Even an old-fashioned non-digital camera is just fine to use when beginning your hobby in photography. If you have always wanted to try photography as a hobby but didn't know quite how to approach it, then start out small. Start by going into your back yard and focusing your camera on a single object, like a solitary flower. Try to capture its essence by taking its photo. There may be different angles that will work for the photo, so be patient and attempt to capture the subject from different angles. If you have a pet, you may want to try taking a photo of him or her. However, some animals get spooked at the sight of a camera, so remember to always be sensitive to their reactions, and modulate your approach accordingly.

Photography can be just as diverse and rich in its complexity as music. And, some photographs have endured the passage of time, such as Mathew Brady's photos of the Civil War, or the photographs that everyone has seen of World War II, or of Vietnam. I once took a trip down to Peru, and was part of an entire crew of travelers. There were people there from all over the world. During the second half of the expedition, we flew down to the Peruvian Amazon, and explored the rainforest. It was, as one of my fellow travelers put, the Real McCoy. I made the choice to take black and white photos of that part of the trip. They were striking. It was the perfect decision to make for that trip. Besides, the canopy was almost entirely green, so it was not as if I was neglecting to capture the rich diversity of color, as you might find in an arboretum, or even an ordinary garden in a residential front yard. I suppose that very good photos could have been taken with color film, but it was one of my first attempts at doing something creative or artsy.

If you continue to practice taking photos, you may very well be able to submit them to journals or magazines. This is what has motivated countless amateur astronomers. Whenever a comet or very bright meteor streaks through the sky, they are usually quick to take good quality photos, and those are the ones that end up in some astronomy magazines. But, I believe that travel still represents one of the best ways to practice your skill with a camera. The next time you find yourself at the beach, or by a lake, or some other natural forms of beauty, such as a mountain, try taking some photos and experiment with different styles or techniques. Perhaps you may find that you enjoy nighttime photography more. Or, you might discover that you enjoy photographing animals rather than people. Give it a try. You may end up surprising yourself.

CREATE A SCRAP BOOK

A scrap book is a wonderful way of being able to record memories along with trinkets that are associated with those memories. And, what's fun about scrap books is that there is no set rule, or method, to making them. It's up to your own imagination. If you celebrated Christmas with family members and friends, you may want to preserve the memories by printing some of the best photos and inserting them into an album. However, don't stop there. You may want to insert some of the Christmas cards you received and have them open-faced. If some of the Christmas presents came wrapped in very pretty paper, then you might want to cut out a small square of that paper and insert it into the scrapbook. The sky is the limit!

Perhaps you may want to place little descriptions next to each photo, and explain what is happening, so that when other people are viewing your scrap book, they will know what is happening. And, family gatherings normally have some funny or noteworthy occurrences. Perhaps someone got sick from too much eggnog, or someone slipped on the snow in the front porch and broke their coccyx. Some family members tend to be more flamboyant than others. You may want to take photos of an uncle as he's standing up and singing, and then later paste that photo into your scrap book. If someone baked really good cookies, paste a 3" by 5" index card with the recipe inside the scrap book, perhaps next to the person who made the cookies. Perhaps you found a very nice winter leaf on the ground. In it goes!

The purpose of a scrap book is to record memories, but doing so in a way that goes beyond just photographs. There's nothing wrong with a photo album. They are among some of my most prized and valued possessions. However, what draws many people to the idea of the scrap book is the idea of being able to include more than just photos. You can place boarding passes from memorable airline flights, or ticket stubs from a movie, or from a rock concert. Dinner menus can be glued on, as can leaves, coins, small rocks, bottle caps, and other small trinkets that have come to be associated with a very memorable event. You can also choose the type of style and colors that will define your scrap book. Furthermore, the entire family can pitch in and contribute their favorite items with which to commemorate an event. And, once completed, the scrap book can become a family heirloom.

TRY DRAWING

Drawing can be a great way of capturing an image in your mind and being able to produce it on paper. Drawing is an inexpensive way to express your artistic sensibilities. What's fun about drawing is that you don't need a lot of tools in order to start. All you need to possess is the inspiration to capture an image. It can be anything, such as a landscape, a mountain, or a sailboat cruising along in the ocean. Drawing can also be a way of interpreting an event. Our minds and our imaginations will cause us to remember events in a certain way, and so drawing can be a creative way of giving form to a memory, such as a vacation for which you have very fond memories.

You may have had the experience of lounging on a tropical beach with nothing but two palms tree and a hammock. This may be what you could capture in a drawing, just as you remember it. Or, you may want to draw shapes which you will eventually fill in with colored paints. Therefore, if you have always wanted to produce your own works of art, drawing them first may be the best way of laying out the blueprints. And, what's fun about drawing is that you can erase any "mistakes" and redraw the lines exactly was you want them. Once you have your drawing exactly the way you want it, you can either leave it the way it is, or you can then paint it. You can also add richness of detail by including different shades of grey so as to imply different amounts of light and shadow.

If you are on a strict budget, this can be one of the most entertaining forms of personal creative expression. Give it a try. You can have fun by drawing caricatures of people you know, or perhaps famous people, by exaggerating their features, such as their ears, or their noses, or the space between their teeth, and so on. Some people pay local artists to draw caricatures of them. Or, you may even want to go one step further and draw yourself! And, in the same spirit, you may want to exaggerate some of your features. Perhaps your hair is a tad spiky, thus, you can draw your hair standing straight up, as if you have received an electric shock. The point is to have fun. Let your imagination soar. When it comes to art, the world is yours for the drawing.

SCULPT WITH MODELING CLAY

There is something so wonderfully earthy about working with clay. Clay is made of natural elements and so working with clay represents another way to enjoy nature, as well as your own artistic capacities. I have worked both with air dry clay, as well as the type that has to be baked. Both are fun. I prefer the air dray clay. Whenever I baked my clay creations, it seemed as though the heat caused the *objects d'arte* to become slightly expanded by the heat and would form cracks on the back. That may have been my fault. I may have been too zealous with the heat in the oven. Nevertheless, working with clay is great fun. You can buy a nice tub of it for several dollars, which is quite inexpensive.

When you work with clay, it's as though, for a few seconds, you get to play God. Your hands can fashion and shape the clay into whatever shape you want. It can be anything at all. It can be a Jack O' Lantern, a pyramid, an animal, a volcano, a bust of a famous person, etc. It's totally up to you. One of the most enjoyable activities from my childhood was making homemade play dough, and adding food coloring to the water so as to have differently colored batches of dough. I loved the scent of the flour and salt (it probably made me hungry!) and the feel of freshly made dough. And, because of the high salt content, it would keep for a long time in the refrigerator.

There is something so primal about working with your hands. I'm sure that those who use a potter's wheel are able to enjoy that wonderful sense of tactile creation. When you create something with your hands, it becomes an extension of you. A large rectangle of clay can bring hours of enjoyment to a family with the minimum of outlay. Or, if your budget is very tight, then consider making play dough at home. There are dozens of recipes online for play dough, so there is no need to buy a book to learn how to do it.

SOLVE JIGSAW PUZZLES

What better way to spend a rainy afternoon than to put together a jigsaw puzzle. And, this is definitely something that the entire family can enjoy. I have regularly seen jigsaw puzzles at garage sales. Of course, it helps if the image is of something you enjoy. They are a great escape on a cold, cloudy day. Jigsaw puzzles help train the mind to see the 'big picture.' And, what makes the even more fun and challenging is that they come in all sorts of levels of difficulty and designs. There are the very easy ones that can be done with the minimum of effort, and then there are the much larger ones that can take days and days and require the entire family to complete.

You can even make the activity fun by setting a timer to see who can complete the puzzle the fastest, or set the timer to see if the entire family can complete it within a certain time frame. Or, you can set up a series of prizes for whoever is able to complete one the fastest. Experiment with different designs. Perhaps the Eiffel Tower one time and the Mona Lisa the next. Or, it can be a puzzle with an image of your favorite animal. The sky is the limit. And, once you've completed it, you can set about doing it again on a different day.

Over time, I have found that one of the greatest pleasures in life is being able to keep my mind sharp and quick. A great way to keep the mind sharp and alert is to enjoy 'brain-teasers.' Jigsaw puzzles are one such category of brain-teasers. It's always rewarding to step back and see the countless small pieces that go together to make up the big picture. In a sense, we are all like the small pieces of a jigsaw puzzle. Each one of us is important because we all contribute a small but important piece of the Big Picture. It takes the concerted effort of everyone working together in a spirit of interdependence to create the Big Picture.

MAKE YOUR OWN HALLOWEEN COSTUME

With the economy in the shape that it's in, many people are becoming more and more creative in the way that they celebrate some holidays. Halloween is one of those days. Of course, there are still many merchants who sell the more elaborate "official" versions of Halloween costumes. Take the Indiana Jones costume, for example. With the fourth movie installment of the Indiana Jones franchise released a few years ago, there was a large resurgence in the selling of the famous archaeologist's costume duds, particularly at Halloween time. All of the costume and even well-established clothing manufacturers jumped on the bandwagon. They all began to sell the "official" version of the types of trousers worn by the swash-buckling, whip-cracking hero. High end cavalry twill. And, let us not forget the all-important leather jacket. And, it has be to me made of just the "right" kind of leather. It could run well over two hundred dollars just for the pants and the jacket alone. And, nobody can dress up as Indiana Jones and not wear the hat! Well, that's another one hundred dollars right there. Never mind the boots, which cost about one hundred dollars. With the economy in its recessionary trough, people are beginning to realize that they don't have to always be buying the "official" version of anything.

The truly fun part of Halloween is being able to create your own costume. Why buy a costume for hundreds of dollars when you can make your own and save those hundreds of dollars. I have seen numerous articles online which describe how to make your own Indiana Jones costume, among many others. You don't need a hundred dollar leather jacket, or a hundred dollar fedora hat. The fun part is in going to the back of your closet and being able to find an old pair of chino khaki trousers, or a well-worn fedora at the local thrift store or Salvation Army.

If you have children, they can join in the fun of making costumes for Halloween. You can even make it a kind of "treasure hunt" and see who can find most of the components of a costume, no matter what the motif or design. Some cardboard, glue, some paints, and clothes from the local Goodwill are all you really need. Perhaps you may already have most of the components. But the point is to make it fun. Too many parents overlook the joy that can be found in creative pursuits. When children ask their parents for something, and the parents cannot afford it, so many of these same parents respond very harshly, and do so unnecessarily. Instead of telling their children "I just don't have the money for it!" these parents can, instead, say to their young ones: "I bet we can make one at home that will look even better!" That way, they maintain a more positive attitude, and their children are ultimately taught by example that people can make things at home, instead of having to pay a lot of money for the store-bought equivalents.

MAKE YOUR OWN CHRISTMAS PRESENTS

Every year, I am struck by the naked avarice on the part of merchants who are oh-so-eager to take my money. It seems that everything that can be sold is sold, or the attempt is made to sell it. Sweaters, furniture, cars, appliances, books, and CDs. You name it, companies are dangling these tempting carrots in mid-air, hoping that you'll reach for them while they conveniently reach for your credit card. However, now is the time for you to take back control of the holiday season. As with the suggestion to make your own Halloween costume, the Christmas season is a perfect time to make your own presents. And, besides, you have to ask yourself, is it really necessary to give presents in the first place? Our society pressures us to spend money on things, most of which ends up as clutter, forgotten in the back of the closet, or sold at garage sales. Yet, year after year, droves of people line up at cash registers all across America to spend money they don't have.

If you want to give a gift to someone, give them the gift of food. This way, it can be consumed and nothing is wasted. Perhaps you may want to bake a batch or two of cookies and give them away gift wrapped and tied with a little ribbon, and a small note. Another idea is to bake a couple of small pumpkin loaves and give them away as gifts. Food will always have its appeal. It never goes out of style, and, once consumed, no longer takes up space. If produced and consumed in moderate amounts, there is also no waste, and, in our ecologically conscious times, that's a big plus.

There's hardly an item for the holidays that can't be made at home. You can make your own wrapping paper. One family, well-known for their penny-pinching creativity showed how they create their own wrapping paper. They simply buy a large roll of brown paper, and sponge paint little trees and leaves on the exterior. If you have developed some talent with clay, or paint, you may want to give away some of your artistic creations. Just think how wonderful a gift a painting that you created would look, framed and gift-wrapped! It would also be very classy, and in good taste. Therefore, make a list of the things you can create at home, and then make another list of the people for whom you may want to give a Christmas present, and then match up these persons with the gifts you plan to make. Thus, the holidays can be enjoyed without having to buy into the corporate 'obligations' that normally come with them.

CREATE YOUR OWN FREE VALENTINE'S DAY

Valentine's Day is one in a series of holidays when we are 'supposed' to buy something for someone, and then, if we don't, it's seen as some sort of failing on our part. The list of items includes, boxes of chocolate, bottles of wine or champagne, and greeting cards as far as the eye can see. Corporate America likes to push the guilt as well. If we haven't bought our significant other a present, then we are not 'good' partners. We are then seen as being negligent.

Now is the time to liberate yourself from this corporate maneuvering, and declare your independence from it. Don't give into that corporate mentality! The only reason that corporate America wants you to give into their pressure is that they want your money. They don't really care about your relationship to your significant other. It is not as though we are referring to a marriage counselor or therapist who would have a genuine concern about the stability and health of your relationship. Hallmark wants to increase its revenue. See's Candies wants to increase their revenue.

If you want to celebrate the Valentine's Holiday without giving your hard-earned money to greedy companies, then consider the following recommendation: make the Valentine's Day holiday as romantic as possible by enjoying romantic activities that don't cost any money. For example, do you live near a bluff, or lookout point, where you can watch the sunset? Consider packing a picnic basket with some goodies from your pantry and going to a certain place, like a lake, or the ocean, or a hill overlooking your city, and enjoying the sunset together. Lay out a blanket and share some cheese and crackers and tell your significant other how much he or she means to you. The irony is, the things that really matter to a relationship don't cost any money. Letting your partner or spouse know how important they are to you, or giving your spouse the massage of a lifetime, do not cost any money. If you have children, leave them with a babysitter, and go out and sit, even if it's under a tree, or on a blanket at the beach, and rekindle the relationship to what it was before the kids, and the bills, and the mortgage.

Fill the bathtub with the bubbliest soap at home, and place some candles at the edges of the bathtub, and spoil your spouse by letting him or her melt in a warm, soothing bath. Place a radio or CD player in the bathroom and play some soft music, perhaps classical or New Age music. Most of us have stacks of little Stick-It notes on our desks. Write romantic or sexy notes on a dozen of them, and scatter them in different strategic location. For example, leave a few in your spouse's purse. Or, leave some in your significant other's briefcase. Leave one in each shoe. Leave a trail of them leading to the bedroom, so that when your spouse comes home, you can direct him or her right to where you are waiting, perhaps wearing nothing but a silky bathrobe...The point is, you don't need to spend money to enjoy the Valentine's Day holiday. No company or corporate entity can make your relationship romantic. Only you and your spouse can do that.

MAKE YOUR OWN GREETING CARDS

Countless stores stock up on their greeting cards well before all of the major holidays. Rather than buying these pre-written cards, make your own. Use some cardboard stock paper and either fold it in half, or cut it in half so as to make a greeting card roughly the same size as the ones available in stores. Get a good quality pen and write your own message. Use your words. Don't let Hallmark dictate what you want to say. Draw an image that represents your feelings. Many relationships have buzzwords, nicknames, and other secretive language known only to the two partners. Here's your chance to write your message using the words and expressions that only your partner would understand.

If you want to give your home-made greeting card a really medieval touch, use a wax seal with your initials on it. Wax seals are not expensive and can add a very classy touch to a hand-written letter. Seals add an elegant flair to letters and greeting cards. Your spouse or partner will really enjoy receiving a card that has your initials engraved on a wax seal. It is enjoyable to melt the wax and drip it onto the paper and then to place a seal on it.

Wax seals make a card or letter feel important, or 'official.' They give it a truly personal touch that no store-bought item could ever possess. Wax seals have grown in popularity over the last ten years or so. Perhaps people finally tired of the impersonal feeling that modern greeting cards, or e-cards, create. Pre-printed greeting cards and e-cards represent the impersonal feeling that factory-made and mass-produced items give. There is nothing intimate in a card that was purchased in a store. But a letter or card that is hand-written, and then affixed with a wax seal, brings forth a uniquely personal nature in sharp relief.

LEARN HOW TO CROCHET AND KNIT

One of the things that impresses me when reading about the early settlers and pioneers in America was their absolute independence and self-reliance. They were able to make (and mend) their own clothes, and cook almost all their own meals. Two hundred years later, in our 'modern' society, we have fallen away from these practices. Some of it is plain practicality. If you're raising three children, and work ten hours a day, five days a week, you're probably not going to have the stamina to knit and mend clothing for your family.

Nevertheless, with the economy on the current roller coaster that it's riding, it may not be a bad idea to learn how to crochet and knit. Once you learn how to create a shawl, or instance, you can move on to more complex projects, like blankets. By creating something yourself, you are able to retain a fair amount of control over the size and colors, as well as the type of fabric or material for your crafts. A homemade shawl or blanket can also make a wonderful Christmas or birthday present. The fun part of making something by hand is that you can add the personal touches which are difficult to find in store-bought items. For example, you can stitch the initials of someone's name into a blanket or scarf. You can use the colors that he or she would love.

There are many books at the public library which can teach you how to knit or crochet. However, if you are the more traditional learner who needs to watch someone demonstrating how to do something, then you may want to opt for a class nearby. The Parks and Recreation departments of many cities sponsor these types of classes for people in the community. If you are over the age of 65, so much the better. They may even offer them to you for free! Yet, even if there is a small fee involved in signing up for a class, or for the materials, it's money that is well invested. Once you are able to learn how to create your own blankets, scarves, and other such items, your sense of independence will probably increase. You might then feel that you don't need to run out and purchase corporate America's carrots, dangling enticingly in front of you. The next time you find that you need something, or want to give someone a gift, you will then have the power to make it yourself.

Category IX

The Community

VISIT YOUR LOCAL PUBLIC LIBRARY

I believe that people underestimate public libraries. Not only do most (not all, of course) libraries have a decent selection of books, but they also carry a fair amount of books on tape, or CDs, as well as movies that can be rented for free or for a nominal fee. I could spend an entire afternoon at a local library and just lose myself in the wide variety of tomes that are there, ready for the taking and reading. The whole world can open up to you in a local library. And, of course, we are truly blessed to be in a country where we have so many public libraries.

Almost every major city has a public library. If you have children in primary or secondary school, libraries can be a good and safe place for them to spend the afternoon studying and getting caught up on their homework. On the weekends, public libraries can be a thriftier alternative to renting movies. The library near my home rents movies for free, and, if the movie was recently released on DVD, they might rent it for a dollar. The library that I patronize has nice ergonomic reclining chairs situated next to large, imposing windows, and it's truly a pleasure to sit on a chair with a book and read it until I fall asleep.

Another alternative is to go to a local college or university library. Local public college or university libraries normally have holdings that are incrementally larger than the ones found in local public city libraries. This is to be expected. Institutions of higher learning have to have the most extensive holdings possible in order to support the research and scholarship of its undergraduate and graduate student body. However, if low-cost movie rentals or books on tape are your preference, then a local public library in your city might be the best place to find them. Libraries are offering an incredible public service which we take for granted. I am sure that most people are aware of the fact that many people in many parts of the world do not have the opportunities to pick up and check out a book for weeks at a time as we do here. Therefore, take advantage of this great public service. Public libraries exist to serve you. Go to your local public library and enjoy all that they have to offer you.

VISIT A LOCAL ART MUSEUM

One of the things which I ponder from time to time is: are young people these days being exposed to the arts as much as they ought to be? And, of course, by the arts, I am referring to the full range of arts that can be had: ballet, opera, classical music, theater, and painted art. It is this last category to which I am now specifically referring. Art is able to capture and crystallize the inspiration of the artist. There have been many forms of art through the ages: prehistoric art, early art, Medieval art, Renaissance Art, and finally modern art. No two people may see a work of art in the same way.

In the end, your appetite for art may be very different than mine. But what is important to stress here, however, is that art museums are true treasures in our communities. There are at least three art museums not far from my home. What's great is that I get to enjoy a great diversity in artistic styles and expressions. I recommend that you explore the city where you live to see if there may be more than one art museum. There may only be one. And, perhaps, none at all.

But, my point is to encourage you to explore the great art that can be found in some cities. Many towns and cities host art festivals. It can be a nice (and free) way to spend the afternoon by walking among the different art exhibits and noticing the different styles that artists employ. Oftentimes, local artists can be seen either working on a new piece of art, or answering questions people may have about their displays. Therefore, if you can't find an art museum, it may be a rewarding experience to attend an art festival. In the end, art has the power to move us, and to stir up the emotions in the beholder. Art can transport us back in time, or propel us into the future. That is the power, and the mystique, of art.

Visit a Natural History Museum

History museums are a great way to learn about the history of our world. They normally have dinosaur exhibits, as well as rock and gem halls, and so on. This is another great way to spend an afternoon without having to spend too much money. One practical recommendation that I would venture to give is that you pack some sandwiches and fruit slices and use those for a noonday meal, rather than the museum cafeteria or local eateries, which normally charge exorbitant prices, even for a sandwich.

Nothing quite compares to be standing in front a skeleton of a Tyrannosaurus Rex, and gazing at the enormity of its size. Dinosaurs seem to have a universal appeal to youngsters. And, the opportunity to gaze at gigantic gems in the rock and gem exhibits is also quite remarkable. Museums have the capacity to awaken our sense of wonder about our world. Many museums also host traveling exhibits. Thus, the natural museum in your city might very well be hosting an exhibit on King Tut, or Egyptian mummies.

What I love about museums is that they can become such a wonderful extension of the classroom. I believe that many students benefit from being able to look closely at the very things they read about in history books. I remember that I would get a thrill from being able to stick my hand into hollow portion in the center of a large iron meteorite at the Los Angeles Museum of Natural History. It's one thing to read about meteorites, for example, and quite another to be standing in front of one that weighs several hundred pounds and being able to run your hand over its darkened exterior, and imagine its fiery plunge down to Earth, or imagining the fireball that it created on its way into our atmosphere.

It is entertaining to ask questions, such as: Did a lot of people watch it? Did it make a sound? Was it loud? Did it leave a trail of smoke behind it? Did it create a sonic boom as it entered the lower atmosphere? These are the things which still go through my mind when I see and touch a large meteorite in a museum. And, I believe that our educational system does not encourage a more active link between classrooms and museums. It is a vital link and one that, I believe, allows students to finally understand, or at least better conceptualize, the things they're learning about in the classroom. And, when they see these things 'fleshed out', like a Tyrannosaur skeleton, it suddenly makes the subject a lot less “boring.”

VISIT AN OBSERVATORY

It seems as though there have been quite a few celestial events as of late. There have been a couple of near-misses from Earth-buzzing asteroids, and we (as of this writing) just had a nearly-total solar eclipse. What better way to learn about these happenings than to take the family to an observatory. There you can find all sorts of fascinating displays and models which explain the life of our universe. Observatories are another great way to make the classroom "come alive."

I recently went to Griffith Observatory, and really enjoyed the overhead projection movie which they showed. It was hosted by one of the docents, and he did a marvelous job of providing the narration of how astronomy came to be a legitimate science. The movie which was shown was projected onto the large dome ceiling above us. It takes visitors on a trip back through time, and highlights all of the major astronomers. Astronomy seems to hold a particular fascination for people young and old. There is something truly wonderful about being given a chance to contemplate the extent of the universe, and to take a step back and see the diminutive dimensions of our planet.

Trips to an observatory can be another great way to enjoy some entertainment on the weekend without breaking the budget. As with the other ideas that have been suggested, I recommend taking home-made snacks and meals so as to cut back on the cost of eating at the observatory, or any of the local eateries. What can make the outing even more entertaining might be to later stop at the local public library on the way home and check out some books on astronomy. By doing so, the whole family can learn more about the very things which were mentioned at the observatory, such as quasars, pulsars, black holes, supernovas, and other such celestial wonders. Astronomy makes for a fascinating hobby. I recently witnessed a shooting star that was visible during the day. It is a rare treat to be able to see a meteor during the day. But, that is what makes astronomy so much fun – you never know what the skies may bring!

VISIT A LOCAL ZOO

Even though zoos are man-made, they are a great way to connect with nature. There is nothing quite like the experience of watching a gorilla sitting on the grass, calmly eating a snack, or watching a tiger pacing back and forth in his enclosure. While it is true that most zoos charge admission, it may still be a fun way to spend a Sunday afternoon. Again, what can lower the cost is to take snacks from home.

Children and adults alike seem drawn to the wonders of seeing different species of animals. As with the idea about the observatories, it may be fun to check out some books at the local library on the way home and read more about crocodiles, lions, polar bears, or any such animal that the family finds interesting. Public libraries also carry documentaries on DVD about the animal kingdom. The animal world is a diverse and fascinating universe unto itself.

One fun thing to do is to compare and contrast animal behavior and human behavior. How much have we progressed beyond the animal stage of our development? At first blush, it may seem that we have progressed far beyond the animals. Yet, when watching the news, wars of territoriality and acts of senseless violence can make one wonder just how 'civilized' we are in comparison with animals. Nevertheless, a day at the zoo can bring these questions to the fore and can make for an interesting discussion amongst the family members.

VISIT A SCIENCE MUSEUM

Science museums are a great way to make learning come alive. From Tesla coils to 3D movies, models of the human skeletal system, and robots, science museums are fun ways to make the otherwise dreary practice of book learning fun and engaging for the entire family. One can read about a rainforest, but the experience of walking through a greenhouse with vapor mists floating between the trees, and hearing the chirping of tropical birds makes the experience seem more real.

Likewise, one can read about how rocket engines work, but the experience of seeing an actual rocket motor in a science museum makes it more real and accessible. There are times when science should not just be read about in a dull textbook. Rather, it should be experienced with actual demonstrations, models, and actual specimens of the items being studied (with the possible exceptions of enriched plutonium and atomic bombs!). Science allows us to understand the way our world, indeed the universe, works. It appeals to the left side of our brain, and the more logical, sequential parts of our mind.

If you have the opportunity, I strongly recommend visiting a science museum. Sometimes it's possible to find coupons and other such discounts, thereby making the outing more affordable for a family with children. Make a day of it, and allow your little ones to roam freely through the exhibit, and share the sense of wonder and excitement with them. I have been to museums and have watched youngsters who seemed absolutely enthralled at the experience of being there, only to see the parents, who look bored, tired, or as though they did not want to be there. Join your children in the excitement and share the learning with them. Make the outing to a science museum an opportunity to bond and grow closer with your family.

START A NEIGHBORHOOD WATCH

Over the years, I have heard people say that we have lost our sense of community in the United States. I believe that to a large extent this is true. People leave their tract homes in the morning, work all day, and come home in the evening, and barely get to know the neighbors on either side of their home. Some believe that "good fences make good neighbors" and that, when it comes to socializing with neighbors, perhaps less is more. Although I can understand that to a certain extent, I also believe that neighborhoods feel much safer when the entire city block is united in a common effort to be watchful of the neighborhood and all agree to report anything out of the ordinary to the proper authorities.

This is what the early New England communities had. They were knit tightly (perhaps too much so) together, and any event in the community was a shared event. On the whole, I think that people felt safer as a result of this shared or collective living. Communities were just that - a communal living space and all people in the community shared a set of common values and they agreed to watch over each other's families and livelihoods. Of course, some communities develop some values that become so regimented that if anyone does not fall into line with those values, they become social pariahs, as the stories of Anne Hutchinson and Roger Williams amply demonstrated. Their values and views did not conform to traditional Puritan ideology, and, as a result, they were banished.

Nevertheless, while I am not exactly advocating a return to Puritan ideology (I value freedom of thought, thank you very much), I do believe that a greater sense of community and communal living might allow people in some cities and neighborhoods to feel safer and to feel less cut off from their fellow man. And, the best way to do this is through a community-sponsored neighborhood watch. You may want to get to know your neighbors a little better, and perhaps gently bring up the subject to see how they feel about the idea. They may not be open to it, but, you won't know until you try.

WATCH A PLAY

There is nothing quite like watching an actual stage play. The actors are right in front of you, and the story is being unfolded right before your very eyes. What is so wonderful about a play is that there is less emphasis on wardrobes and sets, and it's focused almost entirely on the script and the characters whose identities are informed by that script. Most major cities have a civic auditorium or theater which hosts stage plays. Or, as an alternate, many local community college and state universities have stage plays and the performers are local college students, many of whom are quite talented.

Hollywood has created a huge industry whose product, motion pictures, represent the culmination of efforts by distribution companies, studio chiefs, actors guilds, thespians, screenwriters, symphony orchestras, directors, directors of photography, editors, producers and executive producers, not to mention the efforts by the studios to publicize and market their movies. However, the stage play represents a more intimate relationship between the actors and the audience.

Stage plays involve the characters and how they interact with each other, and the emotional catharsis that the play creates in the audience. There is no blaring score by a symphony orchestra, no costumes which cost millions of dollars to make, and there are no grand-scale sets, or digital special effects. It's all about human relationships and how they are able to resonate to the psyches of the audience. If you have never watched a play, check out your city's offerings, or that of a local college or university. You may be pleasantly surprised.

Enjoy Public Transportation

One of the highlights when I visit Disneyland is the chance to ride the monorail. It represents a future where public transportation is more freely available, and people are spared the stress of having to navigate through traffic on congested freeways. I certain hope that a future like that is possible. In the meantime, I firmly believe in public transportation. It represents freedom from the stress of driving. I have enjoyed using public transportation when I availed myself of it. It's a liberating feeling to sit back and allow someone else to do the driving. It is my sincere hope that buses, trollies, and trains continue to be built so that more and more people can have the choice to take public transportation to work.

The automotive industry has convinced us that there is no other way to get to where we want to go other than by driving ourselves there. Although the automotive industry may have the right to produce cars, they should not brainwash the masses to believe that there is no alternative to driving. Of course there is! The alternative is public transportation. It may involve the learning of routes and bus numbers, but the efforts are well worth it. By taking public transportation, you will save money on gasoline, prevent wear and tear on your existing vehicle, and you will prevent wear and tear of your own body.

By avoiding the daily stresses and aggravations of having to constantly drive defensively, you will be able to experience a life that is much more tranquil, and much more frugal. For those of you who might want to consider a life beyond spending, make a side-by-side comparison of the amount of money that you spend every month on gasoline, car maintenance and repair, and car washes. Then calculate how much money it will take to utilize public transportation to and from work for an entire month. You may be very surprised at the difference!

VISIT COMMUNITY CENTERS

Community centers are a great service to members of some cities. They have many services for senior citizens and it affords them a place where they can get together and socialize. Community centers sometimes organize social gatherings celebrating holidays or cultural events. This is also a wonderful way for seniors and other members of a community to experience multicultural events. Some community centers may be part of a city's Parks and Recreation department, or it may be a separate entity. Nevertheless, if you know of any seniors, particularly those of a foreign culture, you may want to recommend a community center where they may be able to socialize with others of their own background and thereby feel more involved in their community. Some community centers may also offer low-cost dancing lessons, gentle sports activities, arts and crafts workshops, and even basic computer classes for seniors. This is a wonderful way for seniors to feel valued and to know that they are an important part of our community.

This is where our American culture, which is so youth-centered, can take a few cues from Asian cultures that place a great emphasis on honoring their elders and valuing the wisdom they offer. Seniors are indeed a treasure trove of wisdom, and a community center devoted to them is a good way to honor these amazing individuals. It is a sad fact that many senior citizens feel alone, and many do live very lonely lives. Thus, the benefit afforded by community centers is invaluable in that they allow seniors to co-mingle and socialize in an environment that is custom-tailored to their lifestyle and their interests. Community centers allow seniors to feel that they are loved and valued.

Community centers are a valuable addition to any city. They allow people to mingle and socialize. This is particularly important for the elderly. It's important that people over the age of 65 feel included and part of a larger supportive social network. Without this feeling, many older persons begin to feel isolated, and this can have an adverse reaction to their health. However, by being part of active social gatherings, they can feel as vibrant and as alert as always. Community centers are a valuable addition to any city. They allow people to mingle and socialize. This is particularly important for the elderly. It's important that people over the age of 65 feel included and part of a larger supportive social network. Without this feeling, many older persons begin to feel isolated, and this can have an adverse reaction to their health. However, by being part of active social gatherings, they can feel as vibrant and as alert as always.

LEARN ABOUT YOUR CITY'S PAST

One of the most interesting sets of experiences I have had involved learning more about the history of the communities where I grew up. I had no idea that Seal Beach, California, was one of the cities producing a stage for the massive rockets that took astronauts to the moon. If you find yourself on a Saturday looking for something new or different to do, I recommend heading over to the local public library and checking out books on the history of the city where you live. The archival photographs of some communities are also very interesting. You'll see the forms and styles of dress that people wore a century ago, and perhaps even farther back. Some of the photos show what were essentially untamed towns and villages, straight out of the Old West, or the days of the Frontier. Some of the things that you'll discover might be more sinister in nature. Perhaps your city harbors a dark history of racial prejudice, or perhaps a notorious crime. Who knows?

You'll get to feel like a sleuth who is doing investigative field work while solving a difficult case. And, perhaps it is the not knowing that will make it feel like you are unfolding the pages of history. You will then be able to reconstruct a diverse and intricate back story of a city whose heritage is replete with spooky legends, interesting photographs, and tales of migration and expansion. You will see the effects of a burgeoning population, world wars, and different laws and ordinances. Perhaps you may be living in a college town, and can therefore see the effect that a college or university has had on the growth of the city.

Learning about your city's past is another good way to feel that you belong to that city, and that you are as important to the development of that city as were the previous generations of citizens who made a home in that city. Not only can you then get a clearer picture of a city's heritage, but, by doing so, you may then be in a better position to see farther into the future of that city and be able to lobby for the kinds of changes which you may feel are in the city's best interest. At that point, you can then become a positive agent of change and progress, leading the way to a better quality of life for all our citizens.

DONATE TO GOODWILL OR SALVATION ARMY

One of the most liberating feelings I have had in recent years is being able to divest myself of much worn-out clothing, or clothing that no longer fits me, or fits my tastes. Some clothes simply fade, and lose their color and luster. Therefore, I make it a practice in my home to always have a bag at the ready in the living room. I call it my Collection Bag, and I throw in it all of the unwanted clothes, books, CDs, and other such items that no longer have a place in my life. But, it's an equally rewarding experience to take everything to the local Salvation Army, and to know that others who are slightly less fortunate from me will be able to wear these clothes or read the books that I have read. And, I am able to return home and find that I have more space in my room, and more space in my closet. Years and years ago, I read Simplifying Your Life, by Elaine St. James, and it had a great effect upon my psyche.

The purpose of the book is to show people how they can simplify their lives on many levels. One of my favorite ways of doing this is by de-junking my room and taking these things to the local Goodwill or Salvation Army. Afterward, I feel that I am ready to let go of the past and begin again, and march boldly into the future. By letting go of the things for which we no longer have an attachment, we are able to reduce our daily existence down to only those people and things which truly matter to us. It's a good reminder that one should not get too hung up on "things." In the end, as they say, you cannot take them with you.

By donating to the Salvation Army or to Goodwill, you are not only de-cluttering your home, but you are also doing a good deed. Your cast-offs can become treasure for someone less fortunate than yourself. Just imagine how good it will feel for an individual with modest means to be able to find a warm winter coat which will keep her cozy during the harsh winter season. By donating to the Salvation Army or to Goodwill, you are not only de-cluttering your home, but you are also doing a good deed. Your cast-offs can become treasure for someone less fortunate than yourself. Just imagine how good it will feel for an individual with modest means to be able to find a warm winter coat which will keep her cozy during the harsh winter season.

VISIT A THRIFT SHOP

Thrift shops and Goodwill stores are some of the most underrated places to shop. Many people (and I was one of them) shun these stores as they might seem run-down, or unappealing. Yet, every time that I have visited these stores recently, I am reminded that going to them is like a treasure hunt. You can never tell what you might find in these stores. There are books, clothes, figurines, and other such little treasures in these stores, and they are sold at very low prices.

One of my friends once told me that he buys all of his clothes second hand. And his clothes always look nice. He has made it a point to do this, and he told me that his wife and grown children do so as well. They must save lots money by doing so. The proof is in the pudding. He and his wife travel to France every year, without fail, and they own a home over there as well. Therefore, do not scorn thrift shops! By making it a point to shop in these stores, you can set yourself on a path that saves you and your family hundreds, if not thousands, of dollars.

A thrift shop is a wonderful way to shop for household items at rock-bottom prices. It truly is like opening up a treasure chest and peering inside, hopeful as to what you will find in it. Thrift shops can supply most people's needs for items such as lamps, furniture, clothes, and kitchen items, such as china. It is amazing to see the beautiful and hard-to-find items that can be found in these stores. A thrift shop is a wonderful way to shop for household items at rock-bottom prices. It truly is like opening up a treasure chest and peering inside, hopeful as to what you will find in it. Thrift shops can supply most people's needs for items such as lamps, furniture, clothes, and kitchen items, such as china. It is amazing to see the beautiful and hard-to-find items that can be found in these stores.

SHOP AT YARD SALES

Right after thrift stores, the other place I love to look for treasures are yard sales. What's great about yard sales is that people are anxious to get rid of their wares, and so they will quickly bring down the price of an item just to get rid of it. The sellers probably also want to have less to haul over to the Goodwill store, and so they bring almost everything down to rock-bottom prices. Like with Salvation Army and Goodwill thrift stores, yard or garage sales are like mini-treasure hunts. What is also great fun is to head over to high-end neighborhoods where the well-heeled populations lives, and patronize their yard sales. They will most likely have very nice items for sale and for really cheap prices as well.

A savvy shopper can often find good and interesting books, movies, sturdy furniture, lamps, and items of clothing being sold. What's fun about buying things at a garage or yard sale is that if the item does not please you, or if you become bored by the books you purchased, you can donate it to the local thrift store, knowing that you did not pay a lot of money for it. It's much more of a gamble to buy things brand-new at a store, as you may later regret having spent that much money on the item in question. But, at a yard sale, you won't have to worry about making that kind of mistake.

What's more, you can often find diamonds in the rough at yard sales, items which, if given a proper cleaning and polish, might fetch a pretty penny on a website where people sell their wares. Many people make a lot of money doing this. They comb the yard sales, looking for things that may have re-sale value, and they buy them at dirt-cheap prices. Then, they clean up these items, and make them look new. At that point, they take very flattering photos of the items and put them up for sale on auction website, and make a killing in profits.

Yard sales are much like thrift shops and the Salvation Army in that you can never predict what you will find for sale. People are anxious to get rid of their wares in order to make a quick buck, and they are willing, therefore, to accept offers from the buying public at rock-bottom prices. It will really is a wise choice to buy things second-hand. This way, you can save as much money as possible, and, in this economy, that is a wise choice indeed! Yard sales are much like thrift shops and the Salvation Army in that you can never predict what you will find for sale. People are anxious to get rid of their wares in order to make a quick buck, and they are willing, therefore, to accept offers from the buying public at rock-bottom prices. It will really is a wise choice to buy things second-hand. This way, you can save as much money as possible, and, in this economy, that is a wise choice indeed!

ORGANIZE A CLUB

One of the more rewarding activities that I have enjoyed over the last decade was to put together a writer's club. This was in the heady days right after the publication of my first book. I wanted to meet other writers, particularly those that were my age. And, I managed to do it. I placed as many ads on-line, and found enough people willing to do it. We eventually found a local cafe where we could meet, and we were off! Our group met once a week, and every week one of us would bring something that we had written to be read aloud to the group. That was fun. I was able to meet really interesting people from all walks of life.

What made it interesting and rewarding was that everyone had a different way of writing, and everyone's work was intended for different readers. Therefore, when we read our material out loud in front of the group, there was a great diversity of creativity and style of prose. You may want to organize a club around your hobby. Perhaps you are a champion bowler, and would like to establish a local bowling league. Or, perhaps you are into badminton, and want to meet others who share your enthusiasm for the sport. What matters is that you are able to meet new people and to establish friendships that last, as I did.

A club can be a terrific way to meet other people who share your passions and your interests. As someone who has already done this, I can attest to how rewarding it is to get together every week with others who have the same hobbies. Also, by doing this, you can experience the responsibility of being in charge of a social entity, even if it is a small one. A club can be a terrific way to meet other people who share your passions and your interests. As someone who has already done this, I can attest to how rewarding it is to get together every week with others who have the same hobbies. Also, by doing this, you can experience the responsibility of being in charge of a social entity, even if it is a small one.

CATEGORY X

Cultivating the Mind

WATCH FOREIGN CINEMA

Some of the best movies that I have ever seen belong to the category foreign cinema. European film makers have a totally different manner of telling a story. Their movies have much less dialog, but what little dialog is there is rich, meaningful and expressive. Movies from Europe utilize a lot less music than movies in the States. It gives some of their movies a more somber, 'grown up' look. Your local public library, if it is well stocked, should have some foreign movies available for rent. With a library membership card, they might even be free for rent, or as low as a dollar.

Nevertheless, if you want to do something inexpensive on a rainy afternoon, but don't want to, or can't, spend any money, then try renting a few foreign movies. Try several. You may want to start with one from Italy, and one from France. One of my classmates in college rents foreign movies with her husband all the time, and they love it. What's fun about watching foreign cinema is that you get to study different directorial methods and techniques. Foreign film makers have what may appear, at times, to be a more artistic manner of setting up a scene, and they often comes across more solemn, or more pensive, than many scenes in American movies.

As Americans, we are used to a certain cinematic style of movie-making. By watching foreign cinema, you can study how foreign directors tell their stories. European movies are very different from American movies. They rely less on an overbearing orchestral score, and rely more on dialog. This is not to say that you cannot enjoy the movies that you have always watched. But, by watching foreign cinema, you can add to your existing repertoire. As Americans, we are used to a certain cinematic style of movie-making. By watching foreign cinema, you can study how foreign directors tell their stories. European movies are very different from American movies. They rely less on an overbearing orchestral score, and rely more on dialog. This is not to say that you cannot enjoy the movies that you have always watched. But, by watching foreign cinema, you can add to your existing repertoire.

Go on a Field Trip

Who says that field trips are just for students in primary school? Shortly before I formally matriculated in a four-year college, I took a college field trip organized by one of the local community colleges. They took us to the old Getty Museum in Malibu, years before the new museum opened up on the hill overlooking West Los Angeles. It was very entertaining. The chartered bus was in the college parking lot early in the morning, and it drove us to the museum where we were able to spend most of the day, accompanied by a nice lunch served at a charming Mediterranean-style cafe.

Many community colleges organize field trips like these to local museums or attractions. It can be a great way to meet new people and check out the sights and places that make life interesting in the communities where we live. Look online, or call the community colleges in your area and inquire whether they organize local field trips. Often, this is put together by the branch of the college that puts together their extension courses.

If you have limited funds, you may want to consider brown-bagging your lunch so as to cut down on cost. Although there is a nominal fee involved in going on these field trips, they are very entertaining, and are yet another example of how classrooms are often extended by including trips to places like museums as well as cultural experiences like going to an opera. Make field trips something fun for the whole family. Perhaps you may want to take your children to the local stock exchange, or a local aerospace plant. This can become another way for your children to equate learning with having fun.

In this day and age, everything must be done to make learning as engaging and as entertaining as possible. Make field trips something fun for the whole family. Perhaps you may want to take your children to the local stock exchange, or a local aerospace plant. This can become another way for your children to equate learning with having fun. In this day and age, everything must be done to make learning as engaging and as entertaining as possible.

Study the Heavens

I have recently learned how to use a telescope. I also want to learn how to spot and identify the constellations and notice how they shift depending on the time and season of the year. Weather permitting, nature has given us a great and free light show in the sky in the form of the constellations. Take advantage of the fact that this nightly spectacle is there to be enjoyed. Take some books out of the library and get the whole family involved in figuring out where the Big and Little Dippers are, or where the Constellation Orion is situated.

Astronomy touches so many other disciplines. Thus, from astronomy, one can venture into European history, or the history of the Catholic Church, or space travel and astronautics. From astronomy, one can venture into chemistry, and a study of the different elements that went into making up the stars and the planets. It is very relaxing to sit on a porch on a cool, breezy evening, and look up at the stars and planets. And, it's fun to track how the constellations change direction throughout the year. There are normally plenty of books in public libraries that explain the nature of the constellations, and how to identify them. Once you become proficient at spotting the constellations, astronomy can become a lifelong hobby for you and your family. It's yet another way to connect with nature. And, provided you have the right weather, it's something that can be enjoyed each night.

You never know when you might witness an extraordinarily bright meteor or fireball. Meteors are always entering our atmosphere, but, because the sky is brightly illuminated during the day, we can rarely see them. However, at night, they can create quite a light show. You might get luck and witness a bolide, or fireball, which is a very large and bright meteor which illuminates the heavens and turns night into day for a few seconds. Or, you might be able to see the International Space Station floating by as a tiny white light, no bigger to the naked eye than a bright planet. Who knows, you might even be able to see strange lights which do not fall neatly into any known astronomical category and be among those who have been fortunate enough to witness an Unidentified Flying Object, or UFO. I was fortunate to witness very strange lights in the sky when I was 13 years old and I will never forget the experience. Therefore, keep an open mind when looking up at the night sky! You never know who may drop in on you.

Try a New Hobby

Lately, I have been learning how to create casseroles, breads, and homemade pizzas. Although I was always fond of watching cooking shown on television, I had never quite set myself to the task of cooking. However, now that I have begun to cook more and more often, I find that it is very rewarding, even addicting. What's great about cooking at home is that you are able to maintain complete control over the entire process.

What motivated me the most to cook, however, was the economy. I was paying close to eighteen dollars for a pizza from a local well-known pizza eatery. However, rather than deny myself the pleasure of eating pizza, I can now make it myself, or a fraction of the price. I also save on the gratuity for the pizza delivery driver. And, I dare say, my pizzas are just as tasty as the ones I used to order in the 'old days.' In the end perhaps cooking is not your things. But, there may be other hobbies you have always thought of taking up, such as fishing, pottery, or horticulture. Do it now. Life is truly shorter than anyone realizes. I certainly want to get to the end of my life with no regrets, feeling the satisfaction that I did it all.

Furthermore, you might have to go through a series of disappointments before you find the hobby for which you were truly meant. Or, you may find that you are indeed a Renaissance person, capable of enjoying more than one hobby. That is what gives life its zest and flavor. It's a wonderful feeling for me that I can saunter into my kitchen and cook a great casserole, and then walk over to my computer and write in my customary prose. I also have become a very decent swimmer. Thus, what gives my life its color is being able to enjoy all of these hobbies.

Look inside yourself, and you may be surprised at the talents you didn't know you had! Hobbies enrich our lives. They remind us that there is more to life than work and paying the bills. Hobbies are fun and engaging. But by trying new hobbies, you also get to experience different activities than the ones you are used to enjoying. Hobbies enrich our lives. They remind us that there is more to life than work and paying the bills. Hobbies are fun and engaging. But by trying new hobbies, you also get to experience different activities than the ones you are used to enjoying.

TRY A NEW LANGUAGE

Some people believe that nothing sounds quite as romantic or seductive as the soft, rolling sound of the French language. Or, you may be drawn to the poetry of Castilian Spanish, or to the mysteriousness of Romanian. Learning a foreign language is a great way to study a different culture. And, what's valuable about knowing a foreign language is that it allows you to interact with the people from the very culture you are studying.

When I decided to join the Peace Corps in 2002, I decided that I wanted to serve in a European country. They decided to send me to Moldavia, situated between Romania and Ukraine. Both Romania and Ukraine have fought over land in Moldavia, thus, it contains both Romanian and Slavic cultural influences. Half the people in Moldavia speak Romanian, and, the other half speaks Russian. The rest speak some sort of aggregation of the two. Nevertheless, one of the highlights of my preparation was getting to learn a little bit of Romanian. It is not that far from Italian.

I once read a story about a native Italian who traveled to Romania, and, upon returning to his native Italy, told his compatriots that Romanians have a very odd way of speaking Italian. Once again, public libraries are a great way of picking up language instruction books and CDs. Or, they may have DVDs intended to teach a foreign language. Goodwill and Salvation Army stores are also a treasure trove of language instruction material, often for a fraction of the original cost.

Learning a new language can be an exciting new way to meet people of a different culture. In our interconnected world, and with the Internet, it seems as though the world is getting smaller all the time. Learning a new language will not only challenge your intellect, but it will also challenge your cultural understanding of different ethnic groups. You will be able to travel, linguistically speaking, to exotic parts of the world. It will allow you to feel more connected to mankind.

TRY CREATIVE WRITING

One of the things which I love about the English language is the fact that there are usually numerous ways to express a thought or idea. There is at least one word to describe almost anything. That is what goes to make English such a rich language. Not only can you say or write practically anything, but you can say it in one of several ways. One great way to get your creative juices flowing is to practice creative writing. You may want to start with something like journaling.

Get into the habit of writing what's on your mind. Or, get into the habit of describing something in front of you in as many ways as possible. Start with something like a tree. Start with the obvious adjectives. Is it large, or green? Is it squat, or stocky? Does it tower above everything else around it? Does it reach so high that it touches the heavens, or at least appears to do just that? Some people anthropomorphize things or inanimate objects and give them human qualities, particularly human emotions. So, is the tree you're describing happy and proud? Is it menacing and ominous? Try and play freely with words to describe your world. And, try to describe it in as many different ways as possible.

Also, read your work aloud to see how it sounds. Get a tape recorder and record your voice to see if the words flow as you would want them to flow. Have other people read your work and allow them to give you constructive feedback. Remember, writing is a craft that requires a somewhat thick skin, as there may be detractors and critics who may not be particularly impressed with your writing. A college writing class may be a good way to start your writing career, as an English faculty professor may be the best source of constructive feedback.

Of all my hobbies, creative writing is one of the most enjoyable activities that I enjoy. With creative writing, the sky is the limit. There is no end to the kinds of tales and stories which can be outlined and written. You may want to try your hand at writing poetry. Ten years ago, if someone had told me that I was capable of writing poetry, with rhyme what's more, I would have thought that they were crazy. Yet, I discovered that I could. Try some sort of creative writing. You might surprise yourself!

PRACTICE SPEAKING IN PUBLIC

There is an old joke that, at funerals, most people would rather be in the casket itself, rather than up in the pulpit delivering the eulogy. Public speaking is a very difficult art to master. Yet, getting good at public speaking can do wonders for your self-esteem. One of the ways that I was able to increase my own capacity at public speaking was to join Toastmasters International. They meet every week and allow their members to speak extemporaneously, that is, off the cuff, without any preparation, or study. By getting their members to do this, they give the members a chance to become better at thinking on their feet, and being able to express themselves effectively without any forethought. Of course, the members do sign up to give speeches for which they prepare weeks in advance. These are the speeches where the members can really shine.

Nevertheless, being able to speak in public will give you a confidence greater than you have ever known. Being able to stand at a board meeting, or in front of other club members, or for your church group, will give you an edge, and it's an edge that you will always possess. It may even allow you to get a promotion at work, or to be given greater managerial responsibilities. You never know what it might lead to, but it's a great way to get your point across in almost situation. It will also help you in your personal life.

So many of us do not know how to get our point across in personal situations. We either shrink back from it, so as not to have any sort of confrontation (not realizing that it never has to get to the point of a confrontation), or we go overboard and raise our voices and shout or use inappropriate language and end up allowing the situation to degrade down to the point of throwing a tantrum, like an infant. Speaking in public can be one of the most challenging skills to master. Give yourself plenty of time to master the art of public speaking. One good tip is to practice in front of a mirror. Another is to look just above and beyond everyone's head. You may want to try different styles of public speaking to see which one appeals to you.

LISTEN TO A BOOK ON TAPE

For those of us for whom reading is more of a chore rather than a pleasure, a book on tape or CD is the next best thing. Yard sales, the Salvation Army and Goodwill shops are a great way to find some of the classics on tape. There is hardly a best-selling book that hasn't been put on tape or CD. What makes the experience better is if you enjoy the voice of the reader chosen for the job. And, what makes the experience enjoyable is being able to take the CDs or tapes with you on a trip, or to hear them on the drive to work. Or you can listen to them before going to sleep.

One of the great aspects of adult education is that you get to control the material, the speed, and the medium being utilized in the enterprise. When we are young, we are at the mercy of what our teachers tell us to read and by when. It is very regimented. And, of course, Cliff's Notes are a big no-no. They are considered contraband. But, as adults, we are free agents, and we control how we will continue our education, and what form it will take. You may decide to skip Moby Dick altogether and just read everything by Shakespeare. Or you may want to focus on learning a foreign language. Or, you may want to focus on the sciences. I really want to learn more about astronomy, and if I can find any books on astronomy on tape I will surely take advantage of it!

Lastly, if you own a tape player at home, this may be a great time to find books on tape at rock bottom prices. Since books on cassette tapes are not being manufactured as much as books on CDs (which are most likely also on the decline), this may be the time to amass as many books on tape as possible, and enjoy them on your tape player. This way, you save as much money as possible, and you get the chance to expand your mind as much as possible. And, the great thing about this is that if you don't like the book, or the subject matter just doesn't grab you, the amount spent will have been minimal, and you can feel good that you didn't sink a large amount of money into a book on tape which ended up not being to your liking.

Books on tape can be a wonderful way to enjoy the world of literature on the go. If you have a job that requires you to travel a lot, then consider books on tape, or CD. All of the classics are now on audio format of one sort or another. By enjoying books on tape, you can complete part of your education that may have been left incomplete. Listening to a book on tape may actually give you an entirely new perspective on a book which you had previously considered very dry and boring. By enjoying books on tape, you can complete part of your education that may have been left incomplete.

WATCH CLASSIC MOVIES

I recently watched a couple of Humphrey Bogart movies and I can genuinely say that I enjoyed them. It can be a very rewarding change of pace to watch old and classic movies. With our current movie offerings being geared almost exclusively towards younger audiences, it is rewarding to watch movies that were made at a time when adults were the wooed target audience.

Classic movies can also bring about a sense of nostalgia. Life in America was simpler then, at least when compared to life today. Movies from the 1930s and 1940s show us a world that was more innocent, but not without its fears. A Second World War was looming, but I believe that even then, there was a greater sense of patriotic unity in the United States. Watching some of the classics can bring about some other benefits as well. Many of the grand-scale motion pictures were done which depicted Biblical events. Therefore, if you are a little rusty on your Biblical history, but feel a bit lazy to pick up the large family Bible, watching some of these movies can be a handy way to round out your education of events which took place in Rome and the Holy Land 2,000 years ago.

Watching classic cinema is also a good way to study how movies were made decades ago. There was more emphasis on character development, and less emphasis on special effects. We live in an era when some movies have an excessive or "gratuitous" amount of digital effects (as one person put it) within their attempt at storytelling. We even have dozens of movies that are computerized cartoons, and all we get to hear are the voices of actors, but do not see real people at all. Watching classic movies gives you the chance to return to a time when movies were made with people, and they were about people, and very human storytelling.

As with other suggestions, your local public library can be a great source to find all of these classic movies. If you find yourself faced with a long afternoon and nothing else to do, stick an old movie that you have never seen into your DVD player. Classic movies take us back to an earlier epoch in American history. Methods of acting and directing have changed. Yet, some classics continue to be amazing films, and have held up with the passage of time. It can be a great way to spend a lazy Sunday afternoon.

READ ONE OF THE CLASSICS

It took me a long time to get through Moby Dick, and I truly want to read the book again. Some people have expressed the opinion that our educational system requires us to read the classics at an age when we are really too young to appreciate them. I have come to believe that this argument may very well have some truth and merit. By growing up and maturing, we are able to develop a keener grasp of the complexities of the human condition. And in so doing, we are then able to deploy greater intellectual forces to absorb the multivariate stories that are inherent within many of the literary classics.

Many of the authors of the literary classics use allegory, metaphors, and other literary devices with which to tell their stories. By reading them at a later age, you will most likely be able to detect these devices with a keener eye and a sharper mind. Upon returning to the classics as an adult, you will no longer be as concerned with "just getting through" the classics as you probably were years ago when you were forced to read them. When I was in school, the only way we could get through them was to read Cliff's Notes, which had a prohibition attached to them as strong as marijuana. In fact, I would be willing to bet that someone caught smoking marijuana would be given less of a rebuke than someone caught reading, or copying material from, Cliff's Notes.

Reading the classics at an adult age also underscores the concept of education being a life-long pursuit. I firmly believe in this principle. Our society, by putting a great deal of pomp and circumstance on high school and college graduations, seems to almost imply that after graduation, our education stops. But, we all know that that concept is not really true. Our education does not stop when we graduate from high school or college. Our education continues our whole lives. Even if we never set foot in a classroom again, our education will continue. It is an enterprise dictated by what we learn. That is the foundation of wisdom. Even if the lesson is as simple as learning not to drink and drive, there is a lesson to be learned. And, in the process of absorbing and assimilating that learning, our wisdom, and thus our education, is increased.

Yet again, our public libraries are a great way to get caught up in reading the literary classics that we may have missed (or just didn't care about) when we were in high school. By reading them through adult eyes, you will be reading them with an entirely fresh perspective. It will almost be like reading them again for the first time. Therefore, check out a book by Mark Twain, or Herman Melville, and find out what truly happened to the Artful Dodger, or to Ishmael.

STUDY YOUR ROOTS/GENEALOGY

One of the more compelling personal projects which my partner has begun has been to trace the lineage of her paternal ancestors all the way back to Scotland in the 17th century. Two of my friends at my church are actually related as a result of their shared Scottish ancestry. By researching your ancestry, you can get in touch with your roots. And, in addition to that, you are able to discover your identity, and how your family came to be in its present configuration. You may be surprised to find some unexpected family secrets.

One of my buddies in college, while doing research on his family history, found out that his ancestors had Irish Republican Army involvement. Therefore, you never know what you may dig up. But, that's all part of the excitement of doing this kind of research. It's the unexpected twists and turns that make it fun. You might have ancestors that were excommunicated, or who fought in the American (or English) Civil War. Or, you may find some ancestors who had shady or checkered pasts. Nevertheless, you can bring honor to your family history by doing the research which lays out, once and for all, the lineage of your forefathers.

What's also great fun is that the tracing of lineages involves a lot of historical travel. As someone who has traveled to far-flung destinations, I value the opportunity to be an armchair traveler and read about the lineages of other people. You may have ancestors here in the Americas, but also in Europe or Asia. The tracing of roots involves the tracing of lines across maps and national boundaries. As much as people may talk about all of us being human and belonging to a single race, what makes the tracing of our lineages fascinating is that it involves the crossing of borders and the assimilation of different cultures, languages, religions, and ethnicities.

It has been said that the only true way to know where we are going is to know where we came from. By studying and honoring our past, we can better plot our family's trajectory over the years. Some family histories are fascinating, and they are interwoven with the story of the American frontier. By studying your roots and genealogy, you will gain a better appreciation of how your family overcame odds and triumphed in the struggle to build a better life.

Get to Know a Foreign Culture

When we speak of culture, many of us forget that cultures encompass many things. The most basic components of culture are: language, religion, music, dance, government, lifestyle, modes of dress, food, style of abode, as well as habits and customs. Here in the States, we think nothing of marching into a friend's house with our shoes on, but, in Asian cultures, one must remove one's shoes before entering a home, particularly if one is a guest. By studying a foreign culture, we allow ourselves to journey beyond our own comfort zone and discover what it's like to live as people do on the other side of the world. Not everyone lives as we do, and although we are truly fortunate to have as many blessings as we do, it is a good exercise in humility to remind ourselves that not everyone in the world is as fortunate as we are in the United States.

Getting to know a foreign culture is also part of our inherent education. I remember that, as part of our Peace Corps training, we had to go to cultural training classes which taught us all about Moldavian culture. European culture is at times very different from what we are used to here in the States. For example, in the summertime, people in Moldavia layout a very lavish dinner at a long table and invite family and friends to join. There is a great deal of drinking, feasting, and dancing. It's not something which we enjoy in the States. Here, we enjoy our dinner in a very discrete way, with just our kin present, and it rarely involves a great deal of tipsy dancing. Therefore, by learning about a different culture, you will be able to broaden your perspective on how people live in some parts of the world. While living in this country, with all of its blessings, we easily forget that other people in the world live their lives in a manner that, at times, is very different from what we are used to as Americans.

Finally, getting to know a different culture is a great way to round out your education. Many college students take a summer to study in a different country. This is part and parcel of being a well-rounded college student. Many students also take a Grand Tour after graduation and explore the Continent of Europe. This is their way of celebrating the fact that they have finished their university studies. Being able to study a foreign culture is part of the college experience. So, if you missed out on the chance to study abroad, learning about a different culture can be a terrific way of rounding out your education. By learning about other cultures, you will gain the understanding that, at times, people in other countries live out of a very different paradigm than the one we use here in the Unites States. As with so many other suggestions, a public library can be a terrific source of books on foreign countries and exotic cultures. By checking out these books, one can become a world traveler, without ever leaving the comfort of your home!

PART III

My Own Personal Journey

The journey I have taken has been one through which many of my previous materialistic goals have come into question. Instead, I have been discovering the value of turning inward, and attempting to re-discover myself. Many people have used the term "finding myself" and it has been the target of derogatory humor, such as "Did you lose yourself?" Yet, this misplaced humor is ill-conceived and rather unfair. Many people do lose sight of who they are. They indeed lose their identities. For many people, the person they were in college has been lost for a long time! For many people, this becomes a slow and pernicious process.

For the longest time, I was undecided as to which major I should choose in college. I had read many self-help books, and their psychological spin on reality was always fascinating to me. It had always been apparent to me that self-knowledge, and self-help, were very valuable. However, in order to truly understand their value, one has to be well-grounded in psychology. Therefore, after much debating and agonizing, I decided to declare a major in psychology at California State University, Long Beach, California. The campus was not too far from my home, and it seemed like a reasonable, if not logical, choice to make for my undergraduate education.

College was a real eye-opener, and mind-opener for me. Upon transferring to Cal State Long Beach from Long Beach City College, I was brought face to face with some of the brightest minds that I had yet met. They courses there exposed me to a wide range of angles of psychology. I learned about social psychology, and community psychology, and so on. The professors were, for the most part, very congenial. This is when I truly began to excel in my studies. I began getting straight A's in practically every subject. By the time I graduated, I had only earned one B. And that was in golf. However, it was not just my intellect that was developing; it was my social world as well.

Being the late bloomer that I was, I began dating while in college. It was not a serious relationship, but it was enough to teach me more about myself, and the kind of woman I wanted to be with. Although my dating was taking place outside of the college campus, and was not with a fellow student, it was still incorporated into my collegiate consciousness in terms of the development that I was experiencing as a result of going to college. In other words, the off-campus dating still managed to be absorbed into my total developmental package of university life. I graduated Cum Laude, and it was a sad moment to have that total existence come to an end.

However, I knew that needed more schooling, and that a Bachelor's degree in psychology was a dime-a-dozen. Therefore, I then decided to apply to graduate school. The school I ended up choosing was the University of La Verne, near Pomona, California. Although I had literally breezed through the classes that I had taken at CSULB, I literally hit a wall when I began taking classes at La Verne. The courses there were very difficult, and the chair of our department held very high expectations of our academic coursework. It was a very taxing venture for me. The rigor of the coursework and the grueling duality of having to study for Comprehensive Exams ("comps"), plus the added necessity of having to write a thesis made the last two terms of graduate school a very stressful experience.

At that time, I was also attempting to continue a relationship that was deteriorating rapidly. In retrospect, I believe that it was the incredible stress of graduate school that contributed to the demise of that relationship. As a rule, relationships require work and effort, and it's very difficult to maintain the investment of work and energy into a relationship when so much of one's energy is being expended in the earning of a graduate degree. Something had to give. The relationship gave. I finally earned my Master's degree. It cost me my relationship, but it was worth it.

Upon finishing graduate school, and upon someone's recommendation, I decided to join the Peace Corps. They sent me off to Moldova, in Eastern Europe. It that provided me with an invaluable cultural experience. And, it was the farthest I had ever been from home. However, there were too many conditions of Peace Corps life that I was not ready to deal with. I became homesick, and I was also having a difficult time learning the language. I learned that the pipes freeze in the winter time, and that the Peace Corps volunteers have to show up at their assigned work site sick with winter flu, and grimy from not being able to bathe for days on end. Plus, I learned that I was going to be the only Peace Corps volunteer for miles around in the town where I would be expected to serve for the full two year commitment. And, it didn't help that the town itself was a true relic of the Cold War. It was populated by large tenement buildings that were built with communistic form-follows-the-function style. They were large rectangular buildings of the drabbest nature, and the town itself looked somewhat desolate.

The whole package was becoming much too filled with demerits for me. Therefore, after three grueling months of training classes and cultural immersion activities, and after having been sworn in, and taken to our permanent village sites, I decided to come home. Upon returning to the States, I worked briefly with deaf students at a local university. It was rewarding, but I knew that I couldn't do that forever. At the same time, I began making guest appearances on a local cable television show as a guest. I had never before been on television. Yet, strangely enough, I felt complete comfortable being in front of the camera. It was Father's Day, and so the theme of the show was, predictably, the importance of fathers. Once cameras started rolling, I realized that this was a lot easier than it seems. And, I was quite comfortable speaking extemporaneously. I spoke about fathers, and how important they are in the family. I was invited again and again to come and speak as a guest. I was falling in love with it.

Around that time, I applied to a doctorate program at Azusa Pacific University, in Azusa, California. The program was even more difficult than the one at La Verne. We were truly expected to commit ourselves one hundred percent to the enterprise. After completing my first semester, I realized that a doctorate program was going to be an all-or-nothing venture. Yet, something happened to jeopardize my ability to continue. The bank where my father was working agreed to fund our very own television show. It was to be called Dialog.

The bank agreed to do this as their way of keeping in compliance with the Community Reinvestment Act, which requires local businesses to contribute to the betterment of the communities in which they are situated. This was too good to be true, or so that was how I felt about it then. After spending all of about twenty minutes thinking about it, I realized that I could not continue both a doctoral program as well as finding and interviewing people during the week, and getting them to agree to appear on our show. I ended up leaving the doctoral program so that I could appear on a local television show.

Looking back almost ten years after this happened, I can see now that my decision to leave Azusa Pacific University was one of the worst, if not the worst, career decisions I have ever made. I would have earned a doctorate by now, and my life would be radically different today. And, unfortunately, I did not have anyone to guide me or warn me of the mistake I was making by dropping out of the program. Yet, at the time, I couldn't get past the immediate gratification of being on television. Some lessons do have to be learned the hard way.

Not long after starting the television show, it was suggested to me that I write a book. I had never thought of writing a book before. What would I write about? I didn't consider myself an authority on anything. I thought about it for a few days and decided that there was no harm in at least trying to write *something*. I thought about how I had written my thesis on how minorities face cultural factors that prevent them from climbing the educational ladder. I finally decided to do it. The book ended up being a treatise on how Latinos do not place education at the top of their priority lists due to their own culture, which does not place enough emphasis on educational competitiveness. A year later, I had a finished manuscript. I was fortunate to have it published a year after that.

After the first book, it was suggested to me that I write a second book. I did. Only this time, my language was a little harsher than it was in the first book. The theme was about how Mexican Americans do not push themselves to succeed to their potential. And, finally I wrote a third book, also about culture. After the three books, I was done with the topic. I had been interviewed on television, had articles written on the books, given lectures at colleges and universities, and, finally, had the pleasure of seeing my books being sold on Amazon.

The central message of this book was intended to stimulate a certain amount of doubt in the reader. By doubt, I am referring to the active process of questioning a set of values. However, the values in question in this book are the values that corporate America wants everyone to uphold. Namely, I am referring to the belief that happiness can be purchased. Happiness cannot be purchased any more than it can be sold. Happiness cannot be found neatly wrapped in package in a department store. Yet, these are the very values that corporate America wants us to believe and defend. What is at work is nothing less than widespread brainwashing. Corporate America has managed to brainwash the best of us into thinking that as long as we purchase the wares and cars that they dangle in front of our impressionable eyes, that we will lead happy, contented lives. We've been duped, and led down the garden path.

As long as we pay attention to the slick commercials and eager ads on the radio, television and the Internet, we run the risk of corroding, or, even worse, gradually abandoning our core values. This slow death of the mind causes people to fall for the superficial mindlessness that corporate America represents. High up within the rank and file of corporate America lies the belief that the masses of people can be programmed to believe whatever they are taught to believe. And, sadly, there are some very visible examples of this in history (for example, the Third Reich). However, what is truly unfortunate is that the attempt to beguile people with splashy ads and insistent messages is still taking place up and down on Shopping Avenue. And, mind you, these messages are appealing to Middle America, to consumers with at least a high school diploma, and even those with some college credits under their belts.

My hopes for this book were modest. I never wanted to attempt a crusade. The forces against me are too strong, and too vast. It would be tantamount to an attempt to swim against a tsunami. And, in the end, I have to respect people's right and desire to spend their money any way they wish. And, I certainly have had my moments in stores when the allure of an item was just too strong, and I ended up giving in to the desire to purchase it. When it comes to that level of 'guilt,' there is plenty of guilt to go around and no one can claim absolute innocence. However, in writing the book, my hope was that a certain amount of consciousness-raising could be potentiated, and that an alternative to spending could be presented. I wanted to show that there is an alternative to a lifestyle given over to spending and acquisition. And, my purpose was also to explain to the readership that it is indeed possible to have a life beyond spending and a sense of purpose that rises above material possessions.

Granted, this, like any lifestyle, can be taken to the extreme. I know of one individual who has become so obsessed about saving money that he goes to work with dirty, yellowing t-shirts, and otherwise dingy, stained clothing. I am certainly not recommending this. There has to be a certain level of common sense about this venture, otherwise it reaches these rather off-putting levels of unreasonableness. I certainly value cleanliness, and esteem it as a praiseworthy feature of a healthy lifestyle. Therefore, try as I might to live a life beyond spending, I certainly will make the requisite effort to wear clean clothes to work, and to keep a well-groomed appearance most of the time. Likewise, I will not eat leftovers that are a week old, thank you very much.

A life that is constructed in such a way that it leaves little room for materialism must still take into account a very basic human need for clean clothes, a clean place to live, fresh food, and the ability to bathe daily. I am not in any way advocating that these prerequisites be abandoned. Not at all. All I am advocating is that people begin to question whether they need to buy a new car every few years, or whether they need to eat out every day at trendy restaurants. The need for clean clothes has nothing to do with the habit of buying an expensive latté every morning at Starbucks.

Yet, the trouble lies in the fact that people have trouble distinguishing between an absolute need, such as the need for basic nutrition, with the need for unnecessary niceties, such as having a pizza delivered and having to pay not only for the pizza itself, but also the gratuity for having it delivered. They confuse the basic need for transportation with the desire to trade in a two-year old car for a brand-new car, fresh off the lot. They confuse the basic need for clothing with a shopping spree at Neiman Marcus. It is this blurring of needing with wanting that gets many people to fall into the spending trap.

But what makes this effort at distinguishing between needing and wanting is the presence of a singularly sticky human emotion - vanity. Many people would not be caught dead shopping at Walmart. They want their friends to know that they shop at Macy's or Brook's Brothers. An item purchased at Kmart or Walmart is seen as inferior or less-than. Why this is so, particularly among reasonable, educated adults is beyond me. Perhaps the thought is that the quality of an item will be considerably lower if it is purchased at Walmart. Maybe. Maybe not. If one is to pass judgment about everything being sold at Walmart, isn't that the same as making a blanket statement, or making a generalization? Isn't that rather unfair? Could it not be possible that some things at Walmart are made of good-quality materials or with good craftsmanship? Better yet, is it not possible that a few of the items being sold at Brook's Brothers or Neiman Marcus might be now and then a tad below par in terms of quality or craftsmanship?

This is the perfect moment in time when we as Americans can take stock of the values which we have espoused for so long, and without question. Not only can we question these values, but we must consider the possibility that they are no longer in our best interest to keep. Behavior is informed and guided by our values. If the behavior we manifest is shaped by values that drive us to constantly acquire goods and spend money, then those values may not always be the in alignment with higher, or deeper, values based on love, nature, and a connectedness to our fellow man, or a spiritual connectedness to the Universe, or God.

In the end, it will not matter what car we drove, or what clothes we wore. When we are at the terminal point of our lives, the only things that will matter will be our relationships, and how we loved, and were loved in return. When we are about to breathe our last, what will matter will be the service we rendered through our industry towards the betterment of our planet and the betterment of the lives of those around us. In the final analysis, the success of our lives cannot be measured by the spaciousness of our homes, or the size of our vehicles. It cannot be measured by the incomes we earned, or the amount of schooling that we accumulated. What will matter will be the manner in which we conducted ourselves and our lives, and the substance which comprised the cores of our being. If we give ourselves over to a materialistic lifestyle, there will come a moment at the end of our lives when we will realize that we have lost not only our money to needless items, but that we have lost our very souls in the process. The merchants in our society rob us not only of our money but they also leave us with a spiritual emptiness. A life given over to spending and acquisition is a life given over to a forfeiture of spiritual sensibilities.

Our time on Earth is much briefer than anyone realizes. Each day, each hour, and each minute are precious. If we live out our precious time thinking about the next item on sale that we want to buy at the shopping mall, we give up our sense of perspective of the big picture. This must be tempered by a reasonable concession that an occasional indulgence in a new watch, or nice cologne, does not spell the inevitable death to our soul, or our sense of purpose in life. The purchase of a new shirt does not mean that my spirit is dead, or that my perspective of my life is now permanently compromised. Extremism is not healthy at any level, or in any form. My message is aimed more at those whose entire existence revolves around an axis of acquisition of material goods. It's a slippery slope. A life of occasional indulgences can gradually become a life of incessant spending if it is not kept under conscious control. And, perhaps that is why I decided to write this book. It is a gentle reminder that a life of relentless spending can be the result of a lack of vigilance over one's personal spending. It is also a wake-up call to remind readers that there are higher values to aspire to in life.

This book was written in defense of a life based upon values that look beyond the immediate gratification of material impulses. We are not here to purchase things. We were put on this Earth to contribute to its betterment. Our sense of purpose should always be a sense of contribution. The form that the contribution takes will be unique to every one of us, yet the overriding purpose should be for us to contribute to the betterment of our planet. Some of us contribute by becoming doctors, and others contribute by becoming custodians, whose mission is to ensure clean, sanitary work spaces. Even the 'lowest' of professions has its importance, particularly if it is carried out with a sense of purpose, and with any eye towards an honest betterment of our world.

A truly evolved or mature sense of self contains within it an ability to see beyond the immediate gratification of personal, but non-vital, needs. We all have very basic needs, in a Maslowian sense, such as the need for sleep, food, water and oxygen. We also have a need for shelter, safety and a sense of belonging. However, what I am referring to here is the 'needs' that people feel believe they have. They are not needs at all. Rather, they are fanciful and materialistic impulses which have become mistaken for basic or vital needs. We may all have a need for a means of transportation, but that is very different from a wish to purchase a brand-new SUV. Simply put, they have confused *needs* with *wants*.

Hopefully, by writing this book, I may be reaching a wide audience that is looking to find a life of deeper meaning and substance. It is based largely upon my own inner journey and the circumstances of my life as they became shaped by the recession which began in 2008. I remember earlier recessions, and I am sure that there will be more recessions in the future. However, I was fortunate to experience a recession whose effects were so strong that it went far beyond another storm which I had to weather. It was a wake-up call. The recession of 2008 became a moment of reckoning. I had to look within myself, and perhaps deeper than I had in a long while. I had to take stock of my values, and to question them. There was no choice for me. I was forced to examine my entire way of life. Did I have to eat out as often as I was doing? Did I need to own as many clothes as I possessed? Could I be happy with less? That was the main question that I was asking myself, over and over: Can I be happy with less? That's not to say that I was going to start living a monastic life of constant privation. Yet, it was a time when I realized that I could make do with far less than what I was used to having in my life.

What made this transition bearable is that I decided to make it fun. I decided to make it a personal challenge to myself. Just how much was I willing to give up? Could I get used to having most of my meals being made at home? Could I get used to home-made pizza, rather than having pizza delivered to my front door? Could I acclimate to the idea of not buying any new clothes for several years? Could I get used to the fact that I may not ever have a new car? Could I accept the fact that I may not ever live in a two-story home? Our society continues to drum into our minds that we should, or 'ought', to have certain things in our lives. We can, and should, develop the strength of character to counter these messages. I don't need a two-story home. I don't need cable television. I don't need a cell phone that can download applications of every nature. I don't need a new car, and I certainly don't need a minivan with a pull-down television at the center of the ceiling.

In the end, all of us must decide for ourselves what gives us a sense of meaning, and what is superfluous. No book, no matter how erudite, can tell us how to live our lives. That is for us to consider and construct. We have to live life in order to find out what is important to us. That entails a fair amount of soul-searching. It also features a fair amount of strength of character. In the end, we all have to stand up for what we believe. That means that even if we decide for ourselves that spending money on superfluous goods is what makes us happy, then that is something which we should assert for ourselves. My only wish is to show the readership that it is possible to construct a life whose meaning goes beyond materialism. It is a life beyond spending.